Walter Scot

A True History of Several Honourable Families

Of the Right Honourable Name of Scot

Walter Scot

A True History of Several Honourable Families
Of the Right Honourable Name of Scot

ISBN/EAN: 9783337184247

Printed in Europe, USA, Canada, Australia, Japan

Cover: Foto ©ninafisch / pixelio.de

More available books at **www.hansebooks.com**

A

TRUE HISTORY

O F

SEVERAL HONOURABLE FAMILIES

O F T H E

RIGHT HONOURABLE NAME

O F

S C O T,

In the Shires of Roxburgh and Selkirk, and others
adjacent.

*Gathered out of Ancient Chronicles, Hiftories, and Traditions
of our Fathers.*

By CAPTAIN WALTER SCOT,
An old Souldier and no Scholler,

And ane that can write nane,
But juft the Letters of his Name.

THE THIRD EDITION,
With Elucidations from the beft hiftorians and writers on Heraldry.

———

H A W I C K:
PRINTED BY GEORGE CAW.
1786.

ADVERTISEMENT.

IN this edition feveral notes are given, to vindicate our author in oppofition to fome more modern writers. As a few of the dedications are prefented to gentlemen whofe families are now extinct, it was thought neceffary to point out their reprefentatives: Thofe that are paft in filence, the families either ftill remain and enjoy the fame eftates, or fuch as the editor could get no certain intelligence of. To render the work more complete, an Appendix is fubjoined, in which the defcent of the Family of Buccleugh, from the time of our author to the prefent Duke, is trac'd; and a brief fketch of the public character of that patriotic nobleman attempted. The appendix concludes with Memoirs of that brave foldier and able commander Lieutenant General Elliot, to whofe anceftors Captain Scott prefents fome of his dedications; particularly to the General's father, Part II. page 61.

To the Right Honourable, and generous Lord,

J O H N

L O R D   Y E S T E R,

Appearand EARL of TWEDDALE; fon to Jean
Countefs of Tweddale, who was daughter to
that valiant Lord, Walter Earl of Buckcleugh,
your honour's worthy grand-father.

AS the Graces, the Virtues, the Senfes, and the
Mufes are embled or alluded to your noble
fect; as all thefe have ample refidence in your
honourable and worthy difpofition; to whom then
but yourfelf, being a perfon fo compleat, fhould I
commit the patronage of that worthy Lord, Walter Earl of Buckcleugh; and though I am an un-
literate foldier, have not apparelled them in fuch
garments of elocution, and ornate ftile, as befits
their honours, and eminency of the leaft part of
their excellent worthinefs; yet I befeech your
honour to accept for your own worth, and their
worthinefs; for if it were not but that I am affur-
ed, that your noble difpofition in all parts is fuitable to the in-fide of this book, I fhould never have
dar'd to dedicate it to your patronage: As it hath
an honeft intention, fo hath your breaft ever been
filled with fuch thoughts, which brings forth worthy actions; as it is a whip or fcourge againft all
pride, fo have you ever been an unfeigned lover of
courteous humanity and humility.   I humbly be-
                                                              feech

feech your honour, although the method and ſtile
be plain, to be pleaſed to give it a favourable in-
tertainment; for records and hiſtories do make
memorable mention of the diverſity of qualities of
ſundry famous perſons, men and women, in all
the countrys and regions of the world: How ſome
are remembred for their piety and pity, ſome for
juſtice, ſome for ſeverity, for learning, wiſdom,
temperance, conſtancy, patience, with all the virtues divine and moral. God, who of his infinite
wiſdom made man, of his unmeaſured mercy re-
deemed him, of his boundleſs bounty, immenſe
power, and eternal eye of watchful providence, relieves, guards, and conſerves him. It is neceſſary
that every man ſeriouſly conſider, and ponder theſe
things, and in token of obedience and thankful-
neſs, ſay with David, ' What ſhall I render ?' &c.
Men ſhould conſider why God hath given them a
being in this life. No man is owner of himſelf.
My age is ſeventy-three; it is fifty-ſeven years
ſince I went to Holland with your honourable
grand-father, Walter Earl of Buckcleugh, in the
year 1629. I was at that time not full ſixteen
years of age, or capable to carry arms in ſo much
a renowned regiment or company as his honour's
was; I was in no more eſtimation than a boy, yet
waited upon a gentleman in his honour's own company; notwithſtanding it is known, that I am a
gentleman by parentage, but my fathers having
dilapidate and engaged their eſtate by cautionry,
having many children, was not in a capacity to
educate us at ſchool after the death of my grand-
father, Sir Robert Scot of Thirlſtone; my father
living in a highland in Eſdail-muir, and having no
rent

rent at that time, nor means to bring us up, except some bestial; wherefore, in stead of breeding of me at schools, they put me to attend beasts in the field; but I gave them the short cut at last, and left the kine in the corn, and went as aforesaid; and ever since that time I have continued a soldier abroad, and at home, till within these few years that I am become so infirm and decriped with the gout, which hath so unabled me, that I am not able, neither to do the king nor myself service; so this being entered into my consideration, it is sufficiently known that my intention and meaning was not to make any profit to myself; for I know I do but little deserve, by reason I could never write a line in my life; neither will my ability keep one to write to me; and I living two or three mile from a school; yet is constrain'd by my own wilful will, sometimes to hire one school-boy, and sometimes another, yet knows not whether they can spell true Scots or not, by reason I cannot read their hand, and there is none by me that can; for many times the writer mistakes the word from my deliverance; Therefore I hope your honour will excuse the failing of my unlearned muse.

Seek then Heaven's kingdom, and things that
    are right,
And all things else shall be upon the cast;
Holy days of joy shall never turn to night,
Thy blessed state shall everlasting last.
Live still as ever in thy Maker's sight,
And let repentance purge your vices past.
                    Remember

Remember you muſt drink of death's ſharp cup,
And of your ſtewardſhip account give up.
Had you the beauty of fair Abſalom,
Or did your ſtrength the ſtrength of Sampſon paſs:
Or could your wiſdom match wiſe Solomon,
Or might your riches Craeſus wealth ſurpaſs:
Or were your pomp beyond great Babylon,
The proudeſt monarchy that ever was;
Yet beauty, wiſdom, riches, ſtrength, and ſtate,
Age, death, and time will ſpoil and ruin it.
Health, happineſs, and all felicity,
Unto the end may your attendance be.

Your honour's moſt obedient,

Humble, and devoted ſervant,

W A L T E R S C O T.

A

TRUE HISTORY

OF SEVERAL

HONOURABLE FAMILIES

OF THE RIGHT HONOURABLE

NAME OF SCOTT, &c.

———————

I WAS once a man, tho' now I'm but a poor
    decriped one ;
Fifty feven years arms did I bear, abroad or in Scot-
    land.
When I began on the twenty ninth, I was a flen-
    der man,
Now when I end on the eighty eight, I am not
    very ftrong.
I never was an hour at fchool, although thefe
    lines I dite,
I never learn'd the catechifin, and now I none can
    write,
Except the letters of my name which I fcarcely
    underftand,
Thefe I was forc'd to learn for fhame when I
    was in command.

A   OF

Adv. Bib.

OF ſhepherd ſwains I mind to carp,
And valiant Tammerlane into the ſecond part,
My drowſie muſe is almoſt drown'd with care,
How ſhe dare venture to climb Honour's ſtair:
The honour's little worth that's purchas'd by coin,
Joan made ſuch a market when ſhe was Pope of Rome.
Honour hath gilded wings, and ſoars moſt high,
And does behold the ſteps of Majeſty;
Honour's the lofty lion of renown,
Which is no merchandize for butcher or clown:
Honour's the greateſt favour a Prince can yield,
All true gain'd honour's won into the field;
He needs no complementing book him to inſtruct,
That gains his honour by valour and conduct;
' Peaſant bought honour is like to thoſe,
' That put a gold ring in a broad-ſow's noſe;
Whereas other metal may ſerve as well,
Either copper, braſs, iron, or ſteel;
I wiſh true honour ſtill may be preſerv'd;
For many get honour that ne'er do deſerv'd:
The valiant Earl of Buckcleugh, when I was young;
To the buſh in Brabant with his regiment came,
Which is the ſpace of fifty nine years agone,
' I ſaw him in his arms appear,
' Which was on the ſixteen hundred and twenty
        ſeven year;
That worthy Earl his regiment was ſo rare,
All Holland's league could not with him compare;
Like Hannibal, that noble Earl he ſtood,
To the great effuſion of his precious blood;
The town was tane with a great loſs of men,
To the States of Holland from the King of Spain.
His honour's praiſe, throughout all nations ſprung,
Born on the wings of fame that he was Mars's ſon,
                                The

'The very fon of Mars, which furrowed Neptune's
    brow;
And o'er the dangerous deep undauntedly did plow.
He did efteem his countries honour more,
Than life and pelf which peafants do adore:
' His noble anceftors their memories
' Are born on wings of fame, as far as Titan's rife;
And univerfally they are divulg'd from thence,
Through the circle of all Europe's circumference;
Let their example be a fpur to you,
That you their worthy virtues may purfue.
'They were brave men, I wifh you be fo ftill,
They had good courage guided with good fkill,
Which fkill and courage, fortune, grace, and will,
I do befeech the Almighty to beftow
On you their offspring all, both high and low;
Time hath recorded Buckcleugh's matchlefs force,
By fea or land with valiant foot or horfe;
They made France tremble, and Spain to quake;
The foundation of Brabant they made fhake:
And as true valour did infpire their breafts,
So victory and honour crown'd their crefts,
Of both Walter Lord *, and Walter Earl †;
In the Netherlands they did fo much prevail,

                             I wifh

---

* This Walter, firft lord of Buckcleugh, was exalted to that dignity
by King James VI. 16th March 1606, on account of his great merit and
many faithful fervices. He carried over a regiment to the Netherlands
where he ferved under that famous General, Maurice prince of Orange,
and there gained immortal honour—Douglas's Peerage page 103. This
regiment, carried over by Buckcleugh, was perhaps the firft of our
Scots Hollanders.

† Lord Walter died in 1611, and was fucceeded by his fon Walter lord
Scot of Buckcleugh, who being much in favour with King James VI. was
created Earl of Buckcleugh 16th March 1619. He alfo had the com-
                                   mand

I wish your good intention may contain,
And you may be like them in every thing;
That as your parents were, so you may be
Rare paterns unto your posteritie.
That all your foes with terror now may know,
Some branches of Buckcleugh have beat them so;
True Honour, Fame, and victory attend you,
And great Jehovah in your just cause defend you;
That immortality your fames may crown,
And God may have the glory and renown.

    WHEN brave Earl Walter he was dead and gone,
He left his son Earl Francis in his room;
Who married when he was but young,
' Before he came to perfection;
His age was twenty years and five,
When death depriv'd him of his life;
His familie they were but twain,
He left them in the mother's keeping;
So by experience we see every day,
That bad things increase, and good things do decay;
And virtue with much care from virtue breeds,
Vice freely springs from vice, like stinking weeds.

    SARDANAPALUS King of Babylon,
' Was to his concubines such a companion,
That he in their attire, did sew, and sing,
An exercise unfitting for a King:
These, and a number more his fancy fed,
To compass which his shifts were manifold;
A bull, a ram, a swan, a shower of gold,

<hr>

mand of a regiment under the States of Holland—Douglas's Peerage
page 103.——Probably he succeeded to the command of his father's
regiment. It was this brave nobleman that our author accompanied to
the field, where, tho' he is silent in his own praise, it is beyond doubt he
distinguished himself by his bravery and courage; and on this account,
not through the interest of friends, was promoted to the rank of Captain.

To

To dreadful thunder, and confuming fire,
And all to quench his inward flame's defire:
Apollo turn'd fair Daphne into bay,
Becaufe fhe from his luft did flie away;
He lov'd his Hiacinth, and his Loronis,
As fervently as Venus and Adonis;
So much he from his god-head did decline,
That for a wench he kept Dametus' kine;
And many other gods have gone aftray,
If all be true, which Ovid's books do fay;
' Thus to fulfill their lufts, and win their Trulls,
' We fee that thefe ungodly gods were Gulls:
The mighty captain of the Mirmidons,
Being captivated to thefe bafe paffions,
Met an untimely unexpected flaughter,
For fair Pollixena, King Priamus's daughter;
Lucretius rape was Tarquin's overthrow,
Shame often pays the debt that fin doth owe;
What Philomela loft, and Tyrus won,
It caus'd the luftful father eat his fon;
In this vice Nero took fuch beaftly joy,
He married was to Sporus a young boy;
And Periander was with luft fo fed,
He with Melifta lay when fhe was dead,
Pigmalion with an image made of ftone
Did love and lodge,---I'll rather lie alone;
Ariftophanes join'd in love would be,
' To a fhe Afs, but what an afs was he;
A Roman Appius did in goal abide
For love of fair Virginia, where he died;
That fecond Henry aged, childifh fond
On the fair features of fair Rofamond;
That it raifed moft unnatural and hateful ftrife,
Betwixt himfelf, his children, and his wife;

　　　　　　　　　　　　　The

The end of which was, that the jealous queen,
Did poison Rosamond in furious spleen;
The fourth English King Edward lower did descend,
He to a gold-smith's wife his love did bend,
This sugar'd sin hath been so general,
That it hath made the strongest champions fall;
For Sichem ravished Dinah, for which deed,
A number of the Sichemites did bleed;
And Sampson, the prime of manly strength,
By Dalila was overcome at length:
King David frailly fell, and felt the pain,
And with much sorrow was restor'd again.
Though Saul his foe he no way would offend,
Yet this sin made him kill his loyal friend;
Amon with Tamar incest did commit,
And Absalom did take his life for it.
And Solomon allow'd most royal means,
To keep three hundred concubines,
By whose means to idolatry he fell,
Almost as low as to the gates of hell;
At last repenting, he made declaration,
That all was vanity, and sp'rits vexation;
Abundance of examples men may find,
Of Kings and Princes to this vice inclin'd,
Which is no way for meaner men to go;
Because their betters often wander'd so:
For they were plagu'd of God, and so shall we,
Much more, if of their sin we partners be.
' To shew what women have been plunged in,
' The bottomless abyss of this sweet sin;
There are examples of them infinite,
Which I ne'er mean to read, much less to write,
To please the reader, yet I'll set down some,
As they unto my memory do come.

Now

Now I leave the family, and return again to brave
Lord WALTER, and his fon WALTER Earl in
Scotland, where thefe worthy Lords were born.

LORD of Buckcleugh into the Scots border
' Was high Lord Warden, to keep them in good
    order;
On that border were the Armftrangs, able men,
Somewhat unruly, and very ill to tame;
I would have none think that I call them thieves;
For if I did, it would be arrant lies;
For all Frontiers, and Borderers, I obferve,
Where'er they lie, are free-booters,
And do the en'my much more harms;
Than five thoufand marfhal-men in arms;
The free-booters venture both life and limb,
Good wife, and bairn, and every other thing;
He muft do fo, or elfe muft ftarve and die;
For all his livelihood comes of the enemy:
His fubftance, being, and his houfe moft tight,—
Yet he may chance to lofs all in a night;
' Being driven to poverty, he muft needs a free-
    booter be,
Yet for vulgar calumnies there is no remedie;
An arrant liar calls a free-booter a thief,
A free-booter may be many a man's relief:
A free-booter will offer no man wrong,
Nor will take none at any hand;
He fpoils more enemies now and then,
Than many hundreds of your marfhal-men:
Near to a border frontier in time of war,
There's ne'er a man but he's a free-booter:
Where fainting fazards dare not fhow their face;
Yet call their offspring thieves to their difgrace;

Thefe

These are serpents spirits, and vulgar slaves,
That slander worthies sleeping in their graves.
But if forty countrymen had such rascals in bogs,
They'd make them run like felter'd foals from dogs;
    The Scot and Ker the mid border possest,
The Humes the east, and the Johnstones the west,
With their adjacent neighbours, put the English
        to more pains,
Than half the north, and the three Lothians:
    Yet with the free-booters I have not done,
I must have another sling at him,
Because to all men it may appear,
The free-booter he is a volunteer;
In the muster-rolls he has no desire to stay,
He lives by purchase, and he gets no pay:
King Richard, the second of England sent,
A great army well arm'd into Scotland,
Through Cumberland they came by his command,
And meant to cross the river at Solway sand.
In Scotland King Robert Stuart the first did reign,
'Yet had no intelligence of their coming;
The free-booters there they did conveen,
To the number of four or five hundred men:
In ambush these volunteers lay down,
And waited whilst the army came;
At a closs strait place, there they did stay,
Where they knew the English could get no by-way;
And when the English came the ambush nigh,
They rose with clamours and with shouting high:
Which so terrified the English, when at hand,
That the most part were drown'd in Solway sand*:
                        'Tis

---

* This memorable engagement happened in the year 1380, and is recorded, with some variation, in Maitland's History of Scotland, Vol. I. p. 561.——Maitland's account is, " Talbot, a valiant commander,
                            " assembled

'Tis clear a free-booter doth live in hazard's train,
A free-booter's a cavaleer that ventures life for gain.
But since King James the sixth to England went,
There's been no cause of grief or discontent:
And he that hath transgress'd the law since then,
Is no free-booter, but a thief from men.
 In Queen Elizabeth's reign she kept a strong
  garrison,
At Carlisle, that cinque-port,
Of horse and foot, a thousand men compleat,
The governor was the lord Scroup.
It fell about the martinmas, when kine was in the
 prime,
Then Kinment Willy and his friends, they did to
 England run.
Oxen and kine they brought a prey out of Nor-
 thumberland,
Five and fifty in a drift, to Cannanbie in Scotland:
The owners pitifully cry'd out they were undone.
Then to the governor they came, and seriously did
 complain:
The lord Scroup heard their whole complaint,
And bad them go home again, and no more lament;
For before the sun did rise or set,
He should be reveng'd upon Kinment:
Anon he charg'd the trumpeters, they should sound
 Booty-saddle,
Just at that time the moon was in her prime,
He needed no torch light:

" assembled an army of fifteeen thousand men, crossed Solway Frith,
" and destroyed the counties of Anandale and Nithisdale: whence re-
" turning with a great booty, he was attacked in the night time in a
" pass by five hundred men, who killed many, took a great number pri-
" soners, and carried most of the plunder back."

Lord Scroup he did to Scotland come,
Took Kinment the felf fame night.
If he had had but ten men more, that had been as
  ftout as he,
Lord Scroup had not the Kinment tane with all his
  company;
But Kinment being prifoner, lord Scroup he had
  him tane,
In Carlifle caftle he him laid, in irons and fetters
  ftrong:
Then fcornfully lord Scroup did fay,
In this caftle thou muft lie,
Before thou goeft away, thou muft
Even take thy leave of me;
He mean'd that he fhould fuffer death before he
  went away;
By the crofs of my fword, fays Willy then,
I'll take my leave of thee,
Before that I do go away, whether I live or die.

Here follows how the Lord Buckcleugh affronts
  the Lord Scroup, firft by letters, and then by
  taking him prifoner out of the caftle of Carlifle by a ftratagem.

THESE news came forth to bold Buckcleugh,
Lord Warden at that time,
How lord Scroup, Carlifle's governour
Had Kinment Willy tane;
Is it that way? Buckcleugh did fay,
Lord Scroup muft underftand,
That he has not only done me wrong,
But my fovereign James of Scotland;

My

My fovereign lord King of Scotland
Thinks not his coufin Queen
Will offer to invade his land,
Without leave afk'd and given.
　" Thou ftole into my mafter's land,
" Which is within my command,
" And in a plund'ring hoftile way,
" I'll let thee underftand,
" Ere day light came thou ftole a man,
" And like a thief thou run away."
　This letter came to lord Scroup's hand,
Which from Buckcleugh was fent,
Charging him then to releafe Kinment,
Or elfe he fhould repent;
　" Scotland is not a fitting part,
" I fuppofe England is the fame;
" But if thou carry a valiant heart, I'll fight thee
　　in Holland;
" There thou and I may both be free, which of us
　　wins the day,
" And be no caufe of mutiny, nor invafions deadly
　　prey.
" Our Princes rare will not compare for dignity
　　and fame,
" It nothing doth tranfgrefs their laws what we do
　　in Holland."
　This meffage by a drummer fent,
To the governor lord Scroup;
A frivolous anfwer he returned,
Which made bold Buckcleugh to doubt,
That he muft into Carlifle ride,
And fetch the Kinment out.
　The Armftrong was a hardy name
Into their own country;

　　　　　　　　　But

But like Clim of the Cleugh and little John,
On England they did prey:
Kinment's firname was Armftrong*,
He from Giltknocky fprang;
But Mengerton he was the chief
Of the name of Armftrong.
It was not for their own refpects,
That Buckcleugh turn'd their guardian;
It was for the honour of Scotland,
By reafon he was lord Warden;
He ftorm'd that any fhould prefume
To enter the Scots border,
Either Cornifh, Irifh, Englifh, or Welch,
Unlefs they had his order;
If he had known when lord Scroup did appear,
To enter the Scots ground, he had ca'd up his rear:
But fince he mift him in all Scotland's bounds,
In England he gave him fowre pears for plumbs.
    Thus being vext, he fhews the friends of the
        name.
How the lord Scroup had Willy Kinment tane;
And faid, if they would but take part with him,
He knew a way to bring him back again.
To which demand they prefently did conclude,
They would ferve his honour to the laft drop of their
        blood:
For certainty did prov'd to be a truth,
He'll ftill be call'd the good lord of Buckcleugh.
His friend's advice that he defir'd to know,
Was Howpafly, Thirlftone, Bonitown and Tufhilaw,
And Gaudilands his uncle's fon,
With Whitefiade, Headfhaw, and Sinton,

_____
* According to the beft authors, William Armftrong of Kinmount.

And Gilbert Elliot, he was not of his name,
But was his honour's coufin-german;
Those gentlemen in vote did all agree,
Five hundred to march in his honour's company;
He thank'd them for their vote, and faid, that muft
　　　not be,
Pick me out chofen men no more but thirty three.
At Thirlftone his brethren they did begin,
They being the firft coufin-german,
Both Walter and William was there in brief,
And prefented their fervice unto their chief;
Then Tufhilaw did follow them,
And fent his two fons James and John,
With Mr Arthur Scot of Newburgh,
And Robert Scot of Gilmarfcleugh,
Bowill his brother William did thither come,
And John Scot brother to Bonitown;
So did William of Haining, a valiant fquire,
And William Scot of Hartwoodmire,
And William of Midgap came theretill,
He was grandfir to this laird of Horflyhill;
Walter of Diphope a metal man,
And John of Meddleftead together came;
Robert of Huntly he did not fail,
He came with the Scots of the water of Ail;
So did Walter of Todrig that well could ride,
And Robert Scot brother to Whitflade,
Andrew of Sallinfide he was one,
With James of Kirkhoufe, and Afkirks John;
Robert of Headfhaw himfelf would gang,
He was his honour's coufin-german;
Sinton and Wall, they ftay'd at home,
Kirkhoufe and Afkirk went in their room;
　　　　　　　　　　　　　　Becaufe

Becaufe it was my lord's decree,
But younger brethren they all fhould be;
Some ftout and valiant able men,
They would not ftay at home,
And fome related to my lord would needs go along,
Although my lord to friends had letten't fall,
He would not have a landed man at all;
Yet valiant men they would not abide,
As appear'd by Hardin, Stobs, and Commonfide;
They counted not their lives and lands fo dear,
As the lofs of the leaft title of their chief's honour.
But now I come for to explain,
The reft of thefe three and thirty men;
Satchells and Burnfoot they crofs'd thefe ftrands,
With Burnfoot in Tiviot and Gaudilands,
Hardin and Stobs before I did name,
Now follows Howfoord and Robertown,
Howpafly, he fent out his brother,
And Allan Haugh fent out another;
Clack and Alton did both accord,
To prefent their fervice unto my lord;
Haffenden came without a call,
The ancienteft houfe among them all.
Thus I have gone through with pain,
To reckon the three and thirty men;
Thefe gentlemen were all Scots,
Except Gilbert Elliot of the Stobs,
Which was a valiant gentleman,
And, as I faid before, my lord's coufin-german;
Thefe gentlemen did all conveen,
At Brankfome-gate his honour to attend;
They neither knew the caufe, nor what the caufe
  might be,
Before they came the length of Netherbie;
                          Although

Although his honour's trufty friend's did ken,
Both fome that went with him, and fome that
     ftay'd at home;
They had it on parol under great fecrecy,
And to reveal't was worfe than infamy;
When it pleas'd my lord to ride, no man did know,
What his intention was, and whether he did go;
Except his counfellors, knights and gentlemen of
     fame,
Which paffed not above feven or eight in all the name;
Wherever he went, he had one or two of them,
And for the reft he let them nothing ken.
   But now for to proceed without delay,
Buckcleugh from Brankfome took the way,
Through the woods of Efk in a full career went he,
To the Woodhoufelies which is near to Netherbie,--
And there a while continued he.
He brought wrights along in his company;
And caufed them fcaling-ladders make,
Although the wrights knew not for what;
Both artificial long and ftrong,
There was fix horfemen to carry them along;
In a high career my lord did ride,
To the Woodhoufelies on the border fide;
For Netherbie is in Englifh ground,
But the Woodhoufelies is in Scotland;
There is a long mile them between,
Divided by the river of Efk her furious ftream;
My lord caus'd raife a vulgar report,
That he was only come to hold a juftice-court:
Which caufed fugitives to flie,
Unto the woods and mountains high;

                  And

And for the ladder tight and tall,
'Twas made for the towers of Brankfome-hall;
Though it was made long and ftroug, and moft
    compleat,
To reach Carlifle's caftle's battlement;
Such excufes there was for every thing,
But for's honour's intention there was no din;
Moft privately he his courfe did fteer,
About Chriftmas, the hinder end of the year:
The day was paft before the wrights had done,
Then it was long eight mile to Carlifle town,
The way was deep, and the water ftrong,
' And the ladder was fifty feet long;
The firmament was dark, the gods were not in place,
Them Madam Night did fhow her ebon'd face;
Luna in fable mantle her courfe did fteer,
And Jupiter he no way did appear;
Then fcorching Sol, he was gone to his reft
And Titan had tane lodging in the weft;
Saturn he did rule into that ftrain,
Mars and Venus under cloud remain'd;
Jove's thunder-bolts in fkies did not appear,
Juno mafk'd in fog, the night was no ways clear;
But yet his honour he did no longer bide,
But paced throughout the muir to the river Eden
    fide;
Near the Stonifh-bank my lord a time did ftay,
And left the one half of his company,
For fear they had made noife or din,
When near the caftle they fhould come,
The river was in no great rage,
They crofs'd near half a mile below the bridge;
Then along the fands with no noife at all,
They come clofe under the caftle wall;

              The

Then masked midnight flowth did keep,
And mortal eyes were all inclin'd to sleep;
Immediately they did their ladder plant,
Which reach'd the castle's battlement;
Then up the ladder they rear'd but doubt,
And broke a sheet of lead on the castle top,
A passage made, and in they came,
The Cape-house door they burst in twain;
Then down the stairs they come amain,
Where Kinment fetter'd lay within,
Then with fore-hammers doors they broke down,
Amazing the lord Scroup, and all his garrison;
They hors'd Kinment with his bolts upon a strong
    man's back,
And to the castle top in the ladder they did him set,
The Warden's trumpets did most sweetly sound,
Which put the garrison in a fear,
That all Scotland was come near.
The governor thought the castle had been gone,
He intended for to run and surely to save none;
Then Kinment said, when first here I did come,
Lord Scroup engaged me to take leave of him;
Then with a turning voice he did cry out;
Farewell, farewell, to my good lord Scroup,
Which terrified the English more,
By an hundred times than they were before;
Then down the ladder in haste they Willy gat,
And set him sadle-aside upon a horse's back.
Mean time the trumpets sounded, Come if ye dare,
' They were the last men that came down the wood-
    en stair,
They mounted all with speed, and safely did re-
    turn
The self same way they formerly did come;

      C

          They

They obferv'd neither file nor rank,
They met with the reft of the party at Stenick's
    bank;
Carlifle's dark muirs they did pafs through,
There was never a man did them purfue,
To Lyne's water they come with fpeed,
Then paft the muirs on the other fide;
Then Kinment Willy cry'd out with pain,
And faid his irons had him undone,
The which to his legs ftuck-like burs,
'He never before rode with fuch large fpurs;
They ftay'd for no fmith on the Englifh ground,
At Canninbie they arrived into Scotland;
Without lofs or hurt to any man,
'At Canninbie a fmith they fand;
By that time Aurora did appear,
And Phœbus fpread her beams moft clear;
The fmith in hafte was fet to work,
'And fyl'd the irons off Willy Kinment;
Yet Kinment Willy durft not ftay at home,
But to Brankfome place, he with his honour came*.

                                 The

* As this brave action of Buckcleugh has been applauded
and vindicated by moft of our Scotifh Hiftorians, it is prefumed
that Maitland's account of it, though in fome circumftances
differing from our author's, will not be unacceptable to the
reader: "In confequence of this," [viz. the king's command
that the Wardens on the Borders fhould maintain good neigh-
bourhood and rigoroufly punifh delinquents] "Lord Scroop,
" warden of the weft marches, and the Baron of Buccleugh,
" having the command of Liddifdale, fent deputies to hold a
" day of redrefs. The place of meeting (fays Spotfwood) was
" at the Dayholm of Kerfhop, where a brook divides England
" from Scotland, and Liddifdale from Bewcaftle. Scott of
" Hayning came as deputy from Buccleugh, and the Lord
" Scroop fent one Salkeld to reprefent him. Thefe two, af-
                                       " ter

The lord Scroup afrighted, he did to London hie,
'And to Elizabeth his queen, he formed many a lie;
As that how King James the sixth of Scotland then
Sent to assault her castle with an host of men:

Which

" ter the truce was proclaimed, by sound of trumpet, (as was
" the custom) met, and, after an amicable conference, parted
" on good terms.   It however happened, that one Armstrong,
" commonly called Will of Kinmonth, was in the retinue of the
" Scotish deputy ; him the English had a particular grudge a-
" gainst, on account of his many and notorious depredations.
" Armstrong, having parted with Hayning, was riding home
" by the banks of the Liddle, when one Grainger of Cumber-
" land, whom in particular he had greatly injured, espied him;
" upon this, part of the English who had been at the meeting,
" chased and brought him prisoner to the deputy, who order-
" ed him to be carried to the castle of Carlisle.

   " The Baron of Buccleugh complained by letter to Salkeld
" of the breach of truce, as it lasted from the time of meeting
" to sun-rising the next day ; but he excused himself by the ab-
" sence of Lord Scroop.   Upon this Buccleugh wrote to his
" Lordship, and demanded, that as Armstrong was taken un-
" justly, so should he be set at liberty without any bond.   The
" lord warden's answer was, That without an order from his
" queen and her council he could not comply, as the prisoner
" was so notorious an offender.   Scott, thus disappointed, pre-
" vailed on Bowes (who had again come from England as am-
" bassador) to solicit Scroop for Armstrong's liberty : But the
" ambassador's letters proving ineffectual, James was at length
" made acquainted with the business, and he desired Elisabeth
" to command his subject's freedom.   But nothing being this
" way obtained, the Scots warden, esteeming both his king
" and himself hurt, determined, with his own forces, to set
" Armstrong at large.

   " For this purpose, having prepared every thing necessary
" for surprising the castle of Carlisle, he crossed the river Edin
" two hours before day, with 200 select horse, and coming to

C 2

" the

Which put her garrison in a terrible fear,
And the villain Kinment Willy carried away clear;
Such numbers broke in at the castle top,
And brought Kinment Willy out of the pit;

He

" the foot of the outer wall, ordered eighty of them to apply
" the ladders : But these proving too short, they broke thro'
" the wall by the postern; this done he commanded the rest of
" his squadron to withdraw on horseback to cover his retreat.
" Though the noise alarmed the watch, and they snatched up
" their arms, yet were they quickly made prisoners, and the
" postern was flung open for these who had not yet entered.
" The eighty having thus got admittance into the castle, soon
" brought Armstrong from the chamber where he was con-
" fined, and founded a trumpet, the signal agreed on, to let
" their companions know they had succeeded. My lord
" Scroop and the deputy were both in the fort, and to them
" the prisoner cried, A good night, as he passed their lodgings.
" Buccleugh then immediately released the watch, and would
" suffer no plundering, although all was in his power, and he
" might have carried off the warden and his deputies.
    " By this time however the city had taken the alarm; the
" bells were ringing, drums beating, armour clashing, and a
" beacon from the tower of the castle shewed the country they
" must fly to their arms. Buccleugh upon this commanded
" his party and Armstrong to horse, and rode speedily to the
" Edin, on the opposite bank of which many Cumbrians stood
" in arms to stop him. But he sounding his trumpets, and
" gallantly plunging into the water, they thought it not advise-
" able to attack such determined resolution. So retiring or-
" derly through the Grahams of Esk, then his foes, he reached
" Scotish ground about two hours after sun-rising. This hap-
" pened April 3d, 1596.
    " Intelligence of this affront being soon carried to Queen
" Elizabeth, she was greatly incensed, and Mr Bowes had or-
" ders to insist at the convention, that the peace must be broke
" unless Buccleugh was delivered up to be punished as his

" mistress

He told the queen he thought to flee in hafte,
The city could not ftand, the caftle being loft,
The vulgar being amaz'd in fuch a fort,
It was bright day or he durft open the port:
They had left the ladder ftanding at the wall:
But in hafte they were return'd to Scotland all;
Wherefore in fign and token of my loyalty,
I here complain of Scotland's villany,
And efpecially of that defperate youth,
The Scots warden, he's call'd lord of Buckcleugh.

" miftrefs fhould pleafe. But the baron urged, that he went
" not into England to affault any of the queen's ftrengths, or
" injure her fubjects, but to relieve a Scotfman unjuftly taken,
" and more unjuftly detained, whom yet he did not attempt to
" releafe till redrefs was denied : in confequence of this, he
" had conducted the enterprize in fuch a manner, that no harm
" was offered to any within the caftle, and no hoftilities com-
" mitted. Notwithftanding which, he was willing to fubmit
" his caufe to be tried by commiffioners appointed by their
" majefties, as ancient treaties ordained : and the court was of
" his opinion.

" But Elizabeth not willing to truft her revenge of the in-
" dignity to this iffue, the council of England renewed their
" complaints in July, when it was again determined in Scot-
" land, that the affair fhould be left to the decifion of the com-
" miffioners : and the king now protefted, that he might with
" more propriety demand the furrender of Scroop, as it was
" more unjuft to detain than to releafe one unlawfully taken:
" yet, for continuing the peace, he would not only not infift
" upon that, but would do all in his power to compromife
" matters.

" ——At laft however James was forced to commit his war-
" den to St Andrews, and foon after to fend him to England,
" whence the queen foon permitted him to return." *Maitland's Hiftory of Scotland*, Vol. II. p. 1265, 1266.

The

'The queen caufed her council to conveen,
And fhow'd them how at Carlifle's garrifon,
Late by the Scots fhe was affronted,
For they on her caftle were high mounted :
And broke in at the very top,
And reliev'd Kinment from the pit,
The queen and her council did command,
A meffenger to pafs into Scotland,
To afk King James what was his reafon,
In a hoftile way to affault the garrifon
With fuch an hoft of man of war,
And fetcht away her prifoner :
The King the meffage foon did underftand,
And fhew'd his coufin the Queen of England.
He then defired her Majefty,
She would be pleafed and fatisfied,
And underftand how things are come and gone,
Which of the nations had done other wrong :
To make herfelf the judge, he was content,
And according to their merits fhe fhould give out
     judgement :
For on his royal word he did explain,
Scroup was firft faulter to the Scots nation :
Lord Scroup he did begin to that effect,
To invade our land, and imprifon our fubject :
With three hundred horfe to come into our land,
Without leave of our warden, or any of our com-
     mand :
A very infolent act againft our crown and dignity,
By the law of arms, he doth deferve to die :
Our ftout lord Warden not being in place,
Though Scroup much wrong'd our nation, and
     did him difgrace ;

                                      It

It feems he did appeal him privately to fight,
But like a coward he did his challenge flight:
And fo without our order, he went out,
To be reveng'd upon the bafe lord Scroup:
No more but fixteen men to Carlifle came,
And gave alarm to the caftle and the town,
Wherein a thoufand did remain,
Your Majefty may think he was a ftout captain;
Our prifoner he did but relieve again,
And none of your fubjects either hurt or flain:
We think his valour merits fome reward,
That of your towers and caftles no way was afraid;
We think your governour deferves both lack and
    fhame,
That fuffer'd fixteen men your prifoner to gain:
That governour is not a fouldier ftout,
Who was a thoufand ftrong, yet durft not ven-
    ture out
With letters to fuch purpofe the meffenger did
    return,
And exprefly fhew'd the Queen, fhe being at London.
Her council did conveen, and the decree gave out,
'That Scroup was all the blame of the paffage
    went about:
The Englifh council call'd Buckcleugh a man
    compleat,
'Which did merit honour, he muft be of a heroic fpirit:
Both king and council founded his commendation,
Wifhing for many fuch within their Englifh nation:
Such praifes made the queen her royal majefty
Be moft defirous that bold Buckcleugh to fee.
The Queen fhe wrote to James our King
All and whole the truth of every thing

With

With a fervent defire to fee the lord Buckcleugh.
The king fent for Buckcleugh, this to him did unfold,
Shewing him he muft go fee, by his command,
His coufin Elizabeth, Queen of England.
Buckcleugh did yield to venture life and land,
And do whate'er the King did him command.
A certain time the King did with him confer,
And fhew'd he was a free man, and no prifoner *.
You with your fervants had beft go there by land,
For all you have to do, is to kifs our coufin's hand.
The fixed day when that my lord fhould go,
Was in the month of March, when hufbandmen do
    corn fow.
A rumor rofe, and fpread through the whole country,
How the lord Buckcleugh he muft at London die;
Upon the fixed day his honour went,
Which caufed many hundreds to lament,
Which faid, alas! they were undone,
And fear'd my lord fhould ne'er return again.
The whole name of Scot, and all his friends about,
Maxwell and Johnfton convey'd his honour out;
The Humes came from the Merfe,
And in Ednam-haugh did bide;
A thoufand gentlemen conveyed him over Tweed;
They put him on to Flowden-field,

* We are rather inclined to reject Maitland in this particular, and believe with Satchels that Buccleugh was not imprifoned. It would have
reflected the greateft difhonour upon the King, had he committed his
Warden to prifon merely for doing an act of juftice and vindicating the
honour of his country; and Maitland himfelf tells us, that James was
fully convinced that Buccleugh had done nothing but what was right,
while Scroop had acted contrary to good faith and the laws then in being. At the requeft of his fovereign, the Baron went voluntarily to
London, but not as a prifoner. It is likely that this heroic adventure
made a part of thofe good fervices for which the King, about ten years
after this, created him Lord of Buccleugh.

The

The length of Scotland's ground;
And there took leave, and back again return'd.
Toward London road they did themfelves apply,
Thirllton, Sir Robert Scot, bore his honour company;
No more there paft with his honour along,
But three domeftic fervants, and Sir Robert Scot
    had one:
The day being Tuefday, twenty-four miles they wan,
And lodg'd in Morpeth, into Northumberland;
On Wednefday twenty-four miles they came,
Into the principality of Durham;
On Thurfday they their courfe did fteer,
Thirty-four miles to Borrowbridge in Yorkfhire;
On Friday to Doncafter his honour bade;
Twenty-eight miles that day he no lefs rade:
To view the town his honour did defire,
It being within the county of Yorkfhire;
For as men pafs along the road,
Yorkfhire is fixty-fix miles broad;
On Saturday, twenty-eight miles he went,
To New-wark town that ftandeth upon Trent,
There all the Sabbath his honour did remain,
The town lies in the county of Notingham;
On Monday, he his courfe did fteer,
Twenty-fix miles to Stenfoord in Lincolnfhire;
On Tuefday, twenty fhort miles he came,
To that town and fhire called Huntingtoun;
On Wednefday, his honour did fare,
Twenty-nine miles to Ware in Hartfordfhire;
On Thurfday, he did go betwixt,
Ware and Troynovent in Middlefex;
Troynovent was the ancient name,
King Lud brought it to be call'd London.

He

He did no fooner London gain,
Till it was nois'd among the Englifhmen,
They run in flocks, and did on's honour gaze,
As he had been the monfter flain by Hercules;
The people to their neighbours did cry out,
Come let us go and fee that valiant Scot,
Which out of Carlifle ftoutly took,
Kinment in fpight of our lord Scroup ;—
In Carlifle Kinment did remain,
Whilft this Scot fetcht him out, and had but fix-
    teen men.
At London Kinment Willy his name was better
    known,
Than it was in the Border-fide where his fore-fa-
    thers were born:
But now for to conclude, within a little time,
The good lord of Buckcleugh to the Englifh court
    did win;
That valiant cavalier he came with fuch a grace,
The Englifh wardens ufher'd him to the prefence;
Notice came to the Queen, that bold Buckcleugh
    was there,
Then fhe left her private chamber, and in prefence
    did appear;
The Queen, in modefty, a complement did frame,
Defiring to know the health of his mafter,
Her coufin good King James,—
A fign of war to me appears, and makes great
    variance,
Amongft fuch blades who do invade,
And become league-breakers,
Since ye intrude within our border,
And did affault our garrifon,

                      And

And Kinment reliev'd without order;
Ye make but a fcar-crow of England's Queen,
I thought my coufin James your King,
Should never done his friend fuch wrong;
But this I leave to another time,
He may repent or it be long.

BUCKCLEUGH's SPEECH.

THEN bold Buckcleugh fpoke forth the truth;
And to the Queen he did declare:
His mafter Scotland's King was free of every thing,
It is your Majefty that makes all the jars;
Your Majefty did order give,
As it appears the lord Scroup lately faid,
That with three hundred horfe he would march
      north,
My mafter's kingdom to invade;
And took his fubject there captive.
This will appear to be a wrong,
And in Carlifle kept him in bondage,
Where he laid him into fetters ftrong.
Whilft I have life or any ftrength,
I'll fight for my mafter's dignity,
His captive fubjects to relieve,
By truth it fhall not fail in me:
My royal mafter, and dread fovereign,
I am his Majefty's fubject born,
And to none other prince but he,
To the oath of allegeance I'll be fworn:
Wherever his fubjects are prifoners tane,
If I can relieve them, they fhall not remain.
I never thought of fuch a lawlefs act,
To invade your nation, and your fubjects take

If

If I had don't, your Majefty had ftorm'd,
But unlawful tane, unlawful he return'd ;
When any of your fubjects unlawfully broke out,
I never did intrude like your governor Lord Scroup,
But to your warden I did ftill complain,
Who fent me his malefactor, I fent him mine again.

THE QUEEN's ANSWER.

THE Queen fhe lent attentive ear,
    And of his honour's courage fhe did much
      admire;
My Lord, fhe faid, your fpeech I'll keep in mind,
And anfwer you at fome other time ;
But neither at court, nor council ye fhall appear,
For I conceive you're a refolute cavalier :
At Channel-hall your lodging fhall be there,
Then through our privy-garden to court ye may
      repair,
For your difport when to the court ye come,
Perufe our library, either even or morn,
At your own pleafure what time fo e'er it be,
And for your clearer paffage ye fhall have a pri-
      vate key,
Except our counfellors and officers in charge,
We do not grant to any, but your merits to deferve;
Thrice worthy Lord, your merits do proclaim,
How honour's noble mark is ftill your aim ;
And to attain the which thou holds thy hands to ftudy,
That thy deferts by fame has won thee gain already,
Induftrious loyalty doth ufe, and all men tell,
To aim at honour it levels very well,
And in your trufty fervice fhot compleat,
That in the end he's fure have hit the white ;

               Let

Let fortune frown or fmile ye are content,
At all eſſays to bear a heart true bent,
Though ſin and hell work mortals to betray,
Againſt their malice God hath arm'd, thy way:
When life and land and all away is fled,
Yet thy noble actions is much honoured,
Thy loyal ſervice to thy king doth prove,
That to thy country thy heart is join'd in love;
Love is a dying life, a living death,
A vapour, ſhadow, a bubble, and a breath;
An idle babble, and a paultry toy,
Whoſe greateſt pattern is a blinded boy,
When fortune, love and death their taſk have done,
Fame makes our life through many ages run;
For be our actions good or ill,
Fame keeps a record of our doings ſtill:
By fame great Julius Cæſar ever lives,
And fame infamous life to Nero gives:
Thoſe that 'ſcape fortune and extremes of love,
Unto their longeſt homes by death are driven,
When Cæſar, Cæſar's ſubjects, objects muſt,
Be all alike conſum'd to dirt and duſt,
Death endeth all our cares, or cares increaſe,
It ſends us into laſting pain or bleſs.

  AWAKE, awake my muſe, thou ſleeps too long,
To bold Buckcleugh again I will return,
Expreſſing of the time that he did there reſort,
And his entertainment at the Engliſh court,
For banquets, he had ſtore, and that moſt free,
Each day by ſome of their nobility;
His attendance was by nobles there,
As he had been a prince late come from afar;
The north-country Engliſh could not be at reſt,
While the Scots warden came to be their gueſt.

Six weeks at court continued he,
Still feafted with their nobility;
To the Queen's majefty he made redrefs,
When fhe would be pleafed he fhould go from hence;
The Queen was mute, and let the queftion flide,
Yet wifh'd that he might there abide;
But yet the King of Scots fhe had no mind to wrong,
By reafon that he was her royal dear coufin,
To whom fhe hop'd to prove as kind,
As mother might do, to pleafe his mind;
What miffes are paft, we do declare,
Your King our coufin will unto us repair,
Your mafter our coufin and we will agree,
We have already acquainted his majefty;
But, my Lord, if you will here remain,
Or if you will return again,
At your mafter's hands we'll get you free,
'And here you fhall have a good falary.
He humbly thank'd her majefty,
Showing the Queen that could not be,
For he had fervice in Holland,
And was bound to obey his mafter's command;
It was too much to be bound to three,
So begg'd that he might pardon'd be.
The Queen anfwer'd, My Lord, fince it is fo,
Ye fhall be difpatch'd within a day or two;
And a letter ye fhall carry along with thee
To our coufin of Scotland his majeftie,
Wherein your heroic fpirit we muft commend,
And intend hereafter to be your fteady friend.
Next day fhe call'd her fecretar,
And charged him a letter to prepare,
To his majefty, King of Scotland,
Wherein fhe lets him underftand,

She

She had ꝑꝑ from her former wrong,
By reafon Buckcleugh was a valiant man.
Cæfar and Tamerlan are valiant men, that's plain,
But in their own perfon they ventured not like him;
Regulus and Scipio was fhort of him againft
    their foe,
Moft ftout Buckcleugh with his fmall train,
Scal'd a caftle, and had but fixteen men,
And brought a prifoner with him along,
That was bound in chains and irons moft ftrong,
Mounts to the caftle top fo high,
And cliverly brought him away;
Yet a thoufand men there was within,
Of horfe and foot in the garrifon,
Although it did us much offend,
Yet his courage we muft commend;
The Queen to him the letter gave,
And pleafantly fhe took her leave,
Wifhing him a good journey home,
In hopes no more her caftle he'd ftorm.
Now I do not intend for to fet down,
How that his honour returned home;
But James the fixth that gracious King,
Was well content of his home coming.

NOW FOLLOWS THE ANTIQUITY OF THE
NAME OF SCOT.

SINCE from all danger Buckcleugh was free,
  I muft fpeak fomething of his familie,
That lord Buckcleugh his fame fpread far,
Call'd Walter lord Scot of Whitchefter;

" Some

' Some late ftart-up, bran-new gentlemen,
' That hardly know from whence their fathers came,
Except from red nos'd Robin,
Or Trail Wallet, country Tom,
' The fons of Cannongate Befs,
' That well could play her game;
Whofe labouring heads as great as any houfe,
Thefe calumnizing fellows can ftagger ftare and
    fhame,
And fwear the name of Scot is but a new coin'd name.
Thefe new cornuted gentlemen, why fhould they lie,
' Mr George Buchannan, and Hector Boetius can
    let them fee,
A thoufand years, if I do not forget,
By chronicles I'll prove the name of Scot,
In King Achaius time that worthy prince,
John and Clement Scots they went to France,
In Paris they at firft began,
In Charles the great his time,
To inftruct the Chriftian religion,
And there a college they did frame,
Which doth remain unto this very time;
And he that doth not believe me,
' Muft read Buchannan and he fhall fee;
Some other authors I could give in,
But thefe are fufficient to them that's not blind;
Some fay, they were not Scots to their name,
But only Scots by nation,
Yet Monks of Melrofs they were known,
Which then was in the Picts kingdom.
John Earl of Channerth firnamed Scot,
To die without fucceffion was his unfortunate lot:
Brave Alexander the firft, a King both ftout and good,
John Earl of Channerth married with his royal blood,
                      Before

Before Alexander the firft, his brother Edgar did
    reign,
The firft that was anointed of Scotland king ;
Reverend John Scot he did furmount,
Who was bifhop of Dumblane, and did the king a-
    noint.
Mr Michael Scot that read the epiftle at Rome,
He was in king Alexander the fecond's reign,
Thomas Lermont was firft his man,
That was call'd the Rymer ever fince then ;
And if my author doth fpeak truth,
Mr Michael was defcended from Buckcleugh ;
And if my author ye would know,
Bifhop Spotfwood's book thefe Scots do fhow.
How can thefe randy liars then,
Make the Scots to be a ftart-up clan,
Sure new ftart-ups themfelves muft be,
For ancient families fcorn to lie.
    But for the antiquity of the SCOT,
There's one thing I had almoft forgot,
Which is not worthy of nomination,
Yet to mark antiquity, I'll make relation ;
In the fecond feffion of king David's parliament,
There was a ftatute made, which is yet extant,
That no man fhould prefume to buy or fell,
With Highlandmen or SCOTs of Ewfdale;
Yet Ewfdale was not near the Forreft,
Where brave Buckcleugh did dwell,
According to the old proverb,
They but fell from the wain's tail ;
But when thefe SCOTs did bear that ftile,
King David refided in Carlifle,
Without and infang they difturb'd his court,
Which caus'd the king that act fet out.
        E   Here

Here I fpeak nought but truth, all men may note,
The very true antiquity of the name of Scot.
And now my verfing mufe craves fome repofe,
' And while fhe fleeps, I'll fpout a little profe.

KENNETH the II. king of Scots, fon to king
Alpin, who was fon to brave king Achaius forefaid, who made the league with Charles the Great,
emperor of Germany and king of France, in the
year feven hundred and eighty-feven *. This king
Kenneth, called the Great, conquered the kingdom of the Picts, about the year of grace eight
hundred and thirty-nine, and joined the kingdom
of Picts unto the ancient nation of Scotland. This

* After mentioning this League, or treaty of peace, between
Charles and Achaius, Buchanan, in his Hiftory of Scotland, Vol.
I. p. 207, 208. fays,. " Charles the Great, whofe defire was
" to ennoble France, not only by arms, but Literature, had
" fent for fome learned men out of Scotland, to read Philofo-
" phy in Greek and Latin at Paris : For there were yet many
" Monks in Scotland eminent for learning and piety, the an-
" cient difcipline being then not quite extinguifhed ; amongft
" whom was *Johannes,* firnamed *Scotus,* or, which is all one,
" *Albinus,* for the Scots in their own language call themfelves
" *Albini :* He was the preceptor of Charles the Great, and left
" very many monuments of his learning behind him, and in
" particular fome rules of Rhetorick, which I have feen with
" the name *Johannes Albinus* infcribed as author of the book.
" There are alfo fome writings of *Clement* a *Scot* remaining,
" who was a great profeffor of learning at the fame time in
" Paris."———This quotation puts it beyond doubt that the
firname of Scot is of much greater antiquity than fome modern
writers feem willing to allow ; and alfo fupports our author's
affertion concerning John and Clement Scot.

victorious

victorious king Kenneth the second died in the twentieth year of his reign. The kingdom not being well settled in obedience to the crown, his brother Donald the fifth succeeded him, a very infamous king and a great tyrant; he loft all Scotland to Striviling-bridge, by the Britons and Saxons, the which time the king Ofbridge conquered great lands in Scotland, affifted by the Britons; fo that Striviling-bridge was made marches betwixt Scots, Britains, and Englifhmen. King Ofbridge coined money in the caftle of Stirling, by that the fterling money had firft beginning; he died in the fifth year of his reign. King Conftantine the second, the Conqueror's fon, a valiant king, in whofe time Heger and Hoba, landing in Fife with a great fleet of Danes, committed great cruelty. King Conftantine the fecond came with a great army againft Hoba, and vanquifhed him: The Scots being proud of that victory, and neglecting themfelves, there followed a cruel and defperate battle, in which the Scots were vanquifhed and king Conftantine, with his nobles and ten thoufand of his army, killed in the fixteenth year of his reign. Ethus, firnamed the fwift, fucceeded his father king Conftantine; he died in the fecond year of his reign. Gregorius Magnus, Dougallus's fon, a worthy, ftout, and valiant king, he freed Scotland all again from Ofbridge, Saxons, and Englifhmen, and enlarged his empire to the county and fhire of Northumberland, Weftmuirland, and Cumberland; and confederat with Eleward king of Brittans, and after went to Ireland, and vanquifhed Braenus and Cornelius, after befieged Dublin, wherein was .

their

their young king Duncan, to whom he was made protector, during the king's minority; then returned to Scotland with a victorious army, and brought threescore pledges of the Irish nobility and gentry, under the age of thirty years; he died in the eighteenth year of his reign. Donald the sixth was son to Constantine the second, a good religious, valiant king; he succeeded king Gregory; in his time the Murrays and Rosses invading each other, with cruel killing, two thousand were killed in either party; the king came upon them with a great army, and punished the principal of this rebellion to the death; he died in the eleventh year of his reign. Constantine the third, Ethus's son, succeeded him, a valiant prince, not fortunate in wars, he being vexed with war in the time of king Edward, sirnamed Sinar, of the Saxons kind, and Edlelton his bastard son; he became a Canon in St Andrews, and died in the fortieth year of his reign. Malcolm the first, Donald the sixth's son, a valiant prince, and a good justitiar; in his time, a confederacy was made, that Cumberland and Westmuirland should be annexed to the kingdom of Scotland, and should be perpetually holden by the prince of Scotland of fee, from the king of England, by virtue whereof, Indolphus, son to Constantine the third prince of Scotland, took possession in both Cumberland and Westmuirland: The king died the ninth year of his reign. Indolphus, Constantine the third's son, succeeded king Malcolm the first, a noble valiant prince; he vanquished Athagen prince of Norway, and Theodorick prince of Denmark; he died in the ninth year of his reign, Duffus, Malcolm the first's son succeeded

fucceeded king Indolphus, a good prince, and a
fevere juftitiar; he died in the fifth year of his reign.
Colonus Indolphus's fon, fucceeded king Duffus;
he died in the fourth year of his reign.   Kenneth
the third, fon to Malcolm the firft, a brave king,
and a good juftitiar.   From the death of Kenneth
the fecond, which conquered the Picts, to the reign
of Kenneth the third, we had nine kings in Scotland: I have fet down particularly how long every
king's reign was, IN CUMULO they reigned a hundred and nine years, moft of them, although I
have not expreffed, were killed in the field,
being fo poffeft with war on every fide, what by
Denmark and Norway on the one fide, the
Brittans and Saxons on the other fide, poor little
Scotland had much ado to get her feet holden
among them: For in all that time of an hundred
and nine years, there was but one victorious con-
quering prince, which was king Gregory: fo that
the borders in thefe lands, in England aforefaid, being fometimes under the command of the Scots,
and fometimes of the Englifh, they became fo rude
and infolent, that they would never be governed
before Kenneth the third brought them under o-
bedience to the crown of Scotland; yet they were
never under fole obedience till the reign of Malcolm the third, firnamed Canmor; he difpatched
them all, and gave their lands and inheritance to
others, which were loyal fubjects.

AND

AND now with fleep my mufe hath eas'd her brain,
I'll turn my ftile to rhyming verfe again;
King Kenneth the fecond, that prince of high renown,
He vanquifh'd the Picts, and conquer'd their crown,
In revenge of his father's death, which bafely they
      murther'd,
For which victorious Kenneth mow'd them down,
And annexed their realm under Scotland's crown;
The year of grace he did their crown annex,
Was in the eight hundred and thirty-fix,
Or in the forty-fix, I know not whether,
The kingdoms they were join'd together,
Being the fourth or fourteenth year of his reign;
And e'er the twentieth he did return,
To his mother earth, from whence he came;
His foul and hope doth reach the fky,
His fame to Titans rife did fly.
Donald the fifth fucceeded his brother then,
And loft as much as King Kenneth did gain;
A vitious, odious king, he play'd at fwig,
Whilft he loft Scotland all to Striviling-bridge,
Yet at's beginning he did come fpeed,
And vanquifh'd his enemies on the fouth-fide Tweed;
The Picts that fled among the Englifhmen,
Requefted Ofbridge and Ella, two great princes
      of England,
To move war againft their enemies in Scotland,
Both Englifh, Brittans, Picts, thefe princes brought,
Which Donald vanquifh'd at Jedburgh,
He was fo infolent after his victory,
To the river of Tweed he came with his army,
And two fhips he took with wine and victuals rare,
And order'd every foldier for to have their fhare.
            King

King Donald was given to variofity and greed,
With luft of body, he could ne'er be fatisfied,
The whole camp they had their paramours,
And was full of taverns, of bordels, and whores;
They followed carding, dycing, and contentious
  trouble,
That each of them they did kill one-another.
King Ofbridge having advertifement anone,
Rais'd a new army, and to the Scots he came;
And kill'd twenty thoufand men compleat,
'Without armour, and all faft afleep.
That vile King was taue, as has been faid,
And in derifion through the country led;
At which time King Ofbridge conquer'd much land,
And that the fouthern parts of Scotland fand,
Affifted by the Brittans, fo that he,
Caus'd Stirling-bridge the marches for to be;
For Saxons, Brittans and for Englifhmen,
In three kings reigns they kept that garrifon,
In Stirling caftle Ofbridge did money coin;
From which the Sterling money had it's firft name;
The Scots valu'd not the land did belong to the Pict,
But the lands of Albion Ofbridge did afflict;
There's Galloway, and the Ifle of Man,
Was lands of Scotland fince the firft king Fergus
  came.
So was Kyle and Carrick, all in haill,
Arran through Lennox, with the neither-ward of
  Clidfdale;
The Merfe and Tiviot-dale was Picts lands,
And fo was all the three Lothians,
So was Peebles, Selkirk, and over-ward of Clidfdale;
Nithfdale, and Annandale; with the five kirks of
  Efkdale,
        'Drunken

'Drunken Donald all thefe lands did tyne,
But Gregorius Magnus recover'd them again,
From Gregorie's death, to Kenneth the third's reign,
The borders obey'd neither God nor King;
Kenneth the third lov'd deer, both red and fallow,
'Above all princes fince king Dornadilla:
Hunting was the fport he liked beft,
For all our fouth-parts were wood and forreft,
Except here and there a fummering plain,
Into which his keepers did remain.

MY mufe has been aftray a certain time,
   But now in cafe for to return again;
With the name of Scot fhe's minded to contain,
Becaufe they are her worthy noble friends,
The year of grace fixteen hundred and twenty-nine,
Carlaverock was a garrifon in that time,
Colonel Monro a German foldier he,
Blockt up the caftle both by land and fea,
Into that leigure I did remain,
In Cockburn's company, I was a foldier then;
And my chance was with my command to pafs,
To the Englifh fide call'd Burgh under Bownefs.
By fortune I fell in a gentleman's companie,
Call'd Lancelot Scot, who was moft kind to me;
He fhew'd me his anceftors haill,
Did live into that fpot;
Since Carlifle walls were re-built,
By David King of Scots;
A book he gave to me, call'd Mr Michael's creed,
'But never a word at that time I could read,
What he read to me, I have it not forgot:
It was th' original of our fouth country Scots.

He

He faid, that book which he gave me,
Was Mr Michael Scot's hiftorie,
Which hiftory was never yet read through,
'Nor never will, for no man dare it do;
Young fcholars have pick'd out fome thing,
From the contents, that dare not read within.

He carried me along into the caftle then,
And fhew'd his written book hanging on an iron pin;
His writing pen did feem to me to be
Of harden'd mettal, like fteel, or accumie;
The volume of it did feem fo large to me,
As the book of Martyrs and Turks hiftorie;
Then in the church he let me fee,
A ftone where Mr Michael Scot did lie.
I afk'd at him how that could appear,
Mr Michael had been dead above five hundred year.
He fhew'd me none durft bury under that ftone,
More than he had been dead few years agone;
For Mr Michael's name does terrifie each one,
That vulgar people dare fcarce look on the ftone;
And more it us'd to pay the Saxons a fee,
For ftrangers are defirous that ftone to fee.

That Lancelot Scot he wearied not,
To fhew me every thing,
'And then incontinent to the ale-houfe did return,
'Where we had the other cup and the other can;
There was no caufe of feed.
Lancelot he faid, I was not a gentleman,
That was not bred to read.

But to proceed, he wearied not,
To fhew the original of the border Scot;
He faid, that book did let him underftand,
How the Scots of Buckcleugh gain'd both name
        and land:

F   He

He faid, gentlemen in Galloway by fate,
Had fallen at odds, and a riot did commit;
For in thefe days, as he did fay,
It was call'd Brigants that's now call'd Galloway.
Two valiant lads of thefe Brigants
Were cenfured to be gone;
Then to the fouth they took their way,
And arrived at Rankleburn,
At Rankleburn where they did come,
The keeper was call'd Brydine,
They humbly then did him intreat,
For meat, and drink, and lodging;
The keeper ftood and then did look,
And faw them pretty men,
Immediately. grants their requeft,
And to his houfe they came;
To wind a horn they did not fcorn,
In the loftieft degree,
Which made the Forrefter conceive,
They were better keepers than he;
In Ettrick-forreft, Megget's-head,
Meucra and Rankleburn-grain,
There was no keepers in the fouth,
That could compare with them;
Thefe gentlemen were brethren born,
If hiftories be not amifs;
The one of them called John Scot,
And the other of them called Wat Englifh.

KING KENNETH then a hunting came,
    To the Cacra-crofs he did refort,
And all the nobles of his court,
They hither came to fee the fport;

                                        Of

Of Ettrick's-hew he took a view,
Then to the left hand did him turn,
Where he did fee that forreft hie,
Which then was called Rankleburn;
The keepers and the ftroufe-men came,
With fhouts from hill to hill,
With hound and horn they rais'd the deer,
But little blood did fpill;
A buck did come that was fore run,
Hard by the Cacra-crofs,
He mean'd to be at Rankleburn,
Finding himfelf at lofs.
The hill was fteep, the bogs were deep,
With woods and heather ftrong,
By a mile of ground there none came near,
But footmen that did run;
Then one of thefe two gentlemen
Which from Galloway did come,
Both hounds and deer he keeped near
To the water in Rankleburn:
And then the buck, being fpent and gone,
He on the hounds did turn,
That gentleman came firft along,
And catch'd him by the horn,
Alive he caft him on his back,
Or any man came there,
And to the Cacra-crofs did trot,
Againft the hill a mile and mair.
The king faw him a pretty man,
And afk'd his name, from whence he came,
He faid from Galloway he came,---
If't pleafe your Grace my name is John.
The deer being curied in that place,

Then

At his Majefty's demand,
Then John of Galloway ran apace
And fetch'd water to his hands.
The king did wafh into a dilh,
And Galloway John he wot,
He faid thy name now after this,
Shall e'er be call'd John Scot.
The Forreft and the deer therein,
We commit to thy hand,
For thou fhalt fure the ranger be,
If thou obey command;
And for the buck thou ftoutly brought,
To us up that fteep heugh,
Thy defignation ever fhall
Be John Scot in Buckfcleugh.
By ftrength of limb and youthful fpring,
Fortune may favour ftill,
And if thou prove obedient,
We'll mend thee when we will.

  John humbly then thanked the king,
And promis'd to be loyal,
And earneftly beg'd his Majefty,
That he would make a trial.
My name is John, and I'm alone,
Into this ftrange country,
Except one brother with me came,
To bear me company.
What is his name, then faid the king?
He anfwer'd, his name is Wat;
Ye are very well met, then faid the king,
He fhall be Englifh, and ye are Scot.
At Bellanden let him remain,
Faft by the Forreft fide,

Where

Where he may do us fervice too,
And affist you with his aid.
　　I do believe as my author did declare,
That the original of Buckcleugh was a valiant
　　　　Forrester,
It's moft like to be true which I have plainly fhown,
The old families of Buckcleugh did carry a hun-
　　　　ting-horn;
Buckcleugh, if that my author doth fpeak truth,
It's long fince he began,——
In the third king Kenneth's reign,
He to the Forrest came *.

　　　　　　　　　　　　　　　　　　The

* Kenneth the III. afcended the throne in the year 969, and died in
994. In what year of his reign the firname of Scot was given to the progenitor of the Buccleugh family we are not informed: But there are various reafons for believing that Satchels' account is juft, while the opi-
nions of thofe who differ from him do not appear well founded. The
Uchtred, whom Douglas, in his Peerage of Scotland, mentions as the
progenitor of all the Scots in Scotland, feems evidently to have been a
defcendant of the firft Scot of Buccleugh. His defigning himfelf filius Scot is a proof of this. To imagine that he defigned himfelf filius
Scot to fignify his being the fon of a Scotfman is rather abfurd. Might
not almoft every perfon in the nation, with equal propriety, have defigned
himfelf the fon of a Scotfman? Is it not more rational to fuppofe that filius Scot meant the fon of fome perfon who was then known by the name
of Scot?—It behoved to be fome time before the defcendants of John of
Buckfcleugh became numerous, or fo great as to be attendants at court,
which feems to be the reafon why Douglas cannot find them amongft the
nobility till the reign of Alexander I. who fucceeded to the crown in 1107.
By this time their valour and courage had raifed them to honour and
favour with their Prince, which to the prefent time remain unfullied.—
Though, according to Douglas, the defcendants of the above Uchtred were
firft defigned of Murdiefton, this does not fay, that they were not a branch
of the Buckcleugh family; nor deny, that they might again, upon the death
of fome of their relations, fucceed to the reprefentation of the ancient
family.———The title of the family being taken from the lands of Buckcleugh, in preference to all their other vaft poffeffions, tends very much
to confirm the account given by our author.
　　What became of Wat. Englifh, the brother of the firft John Scot of
Buckcleugh, and his defcendants, we have no account. The following
　　　　　　　　　　　　　　　　　　　　　　　　　　　　con-

The firſt of their genealogy,
Though chronicles be rent and torn,
And made their ends upon the ſea;
Of late into the Uſurper's time,
Our regiſters away were tane,
Many of them periſh'd in the main,
And never came aſhore again.
In Queen Mary's reign they had bad handling,
Sometimes fortune favour'd, and ſometimes frown'd,
'Twixt ſtools, if men do miſs their mark,
Their bottom ſure goes to the ground.
In Edward Longſhanks' time, king of England,
Our monuments were loſt and gone,
Our chronicles and regiſters to London went,
Yet not return'd again.
In the reign of the third Conſtantine,
All ſubſtance from this land was tane,
By that Saxon king Edward ſirnamed Cinar,
And Edleſton, his baſtard ſon;
Since theſe hurli-burlies, tops-a-turvies,
So oft this land they have undone,
That a native durſt not ſhow himſelf,
Except on the tops of the mountains.
When our records were ſent away,
The vulgar ſort they were not free,

conjecture concerning his poſterity is ſubmitted to the reader: Wat's
place of reſidence being fixed at Bellanden, upon the ſouth ſide of the
Forreſt of Rankleburn, betwixt Buckcleugh and Branxholm, it may not
be improbable that the ſirname of Engliſh, given him by Kenneth, might
have been ſome how corrupted into that of Ingliſh and Inglis, both of
which names are pretty common in Scotland, eſpecially Inglis: Perhaps
Inglis of Branxholm, with whom Sir Walter Scot, in the year 1446, exchanged his lands of Murdieſton for the lands of Branxholm, Branſhaw,
Whitlaw, Whitrigs, Goldilands, Todiſhaw, Todholes, &c. was one of
the deſcendants of this Wat. Engliſh

                                              There-

Therefore there was particular acts,
For to be cloaks to their knavery;
The chronicle may err, fome men may be preferr'd,
In every fcience there is fome cheatry;
For if an inferior man to a clerk fhall come,
And poffefs him of fuch gallantry,
Then he'll take a word alone,
And fo reward him with his coin,
Which will caufe the clerk blaze him to the fky,
Within two hundred years may be it will appear,
If the world fhall ftand fo long,
That the late-made Purves act,
Which he obtained to cover his fact,
Will raife his needy friends to be gentlemen.
　But bold Buckcleugh was none of them,
That ever bought his honour with coin,
His valour did it gain in Holland and Spain,
And againft the Saxons feed they oft did honour
　　gain.
From the family of Buckcleugh,
There has fprung many a man,
Four hundred years ago;
Haffinden he was one,
Defcended of that line, and ftill he doth remain,
And evidents fpeak truth, the fame the truth pro-
　　claim.
Though chronicles be loft from many a family,
Thefe characters that remain the truth do let us fee,
Sir Alexander Scot of Haffinden was knight,
With good king James the Fourth he was killed at
　　Flowden fight.
From Haffenden did fpring before that time,
The families of Wall, Delorain, and Haining,
　　　　　　　　　　　　The

The fouth-country gentry it is known for truth,
Were exercis'd to arms in their youth,
None other education they did apply,
But jack and fpear againft their enemy;
And becaufe it was their daily exercife,
' They never fought to be chronicliz'd:
But when a courtier did any valiant fate,
He was cry'd up to th' ftars, and made lord of ftate.
  But now advance, my mufe, and declare the truth
Of brave John Scot, the original of Buckcleugh;
' And becaufe thou art weary, as I fuppofe,
' I'll refrain verfe, and turn myfelf to profe;
Good Lancelot Scot, I think his book be true,
Old Rankelburn is defigned Buckcleugh now;
Yet in his book no Balls read he,
It was Buckscleugh he read to me;
He told me the name, the place, the cote,
Came all by the hunting of the buck:
In Scotland no Buckcleugh was then,
Before the Buck in the Cleugh was flain;
Nights-men at firft they did appear,
Becaufe moon and ftars to their arms they bear,
Their creft, fupporters, and hunting-horn,
Shows their beginning from hunting came;
Their name and ftile the book did fay,
John gain'd them both into one day:
The very place where that the buck was flain,
He built a ftone houfe, and there he did remain;
He built a church into that Forreft high,
There was no man to come to it but his own family;
The houfe's ground-work yet is to be feen;
And at that church I many times have been,
A burial place it yet keeps out,
For any poor folks that lie round about;

'To

To the parish church it's long six-miles,
Therefore they bury yet to save toil.
My Good-sir Satchels, I heard him declare,
There was nine Lairds of Buckcleugh buried there;
But now with rubbish and earth it's filled up so high,
That no man can the through-stones see,
But nine tomb-stones he saw with both his eyne,
'But knew not who was buried under them.
Also they built a Mill on that same burn,
To grind dogs-bran, tho' there there grew no corn,
For in my own time corn little there hath been,
There was neither rig nor fur for to be seen,
But hills and mountains on every side,
The haugh below, scarce a hundred foot wide;
Yet there's a mill-stead in that brook,
And the church-walls I have seen them all up,
It is two reasonable mile
Between the mill-stead and the kirk-style;
My Good-sir told me there he had seen,
A holy cross, and a font-stone;
The parish being twenty-mile about,
But hardly sixteen folks remain in it.
All the corn I have seen there in a year,
Was scarce the sowing of six firlots of bear;
And for neighbours to come with good will,
There was no corn to grind into that mill,
'If heather-tops had been meal of the best,
'Then Buckcleugh-mill had gotten a noble grift.
Now wearied muse to rest thou mayst resort,
'Whilst I a little prose report.

G   I heard

I Heard my Good-fir tell, that he heard all men fay, the reafon why the lairds of Buckcleugh did build that mill was for the ufe of their houfes, for grinding of flour, meal, and malt, but efpecially bran for their dogs, and the corn came out of other barronies, which was then in his poffeffion; as the Ewards in Tweedale, the barròny of Eckfoord, Grimflies in Eaft-Tiviotdale, and other barronies and lands under his command; this is fpoken by tradition to this time. But fure if fuch things were, as it hath been by all appearance, it muft have been long after the beginning of the honourable family of Buckcleugh; for at that time Buckcleugh muft needs be a perfon of much honour and renown, and of a very competent eftate, when he built a church and a mill in fuch a wild Forreft as Rankleburn, now called Buckcleugh, where there was no people to come to the church, except his own family, nor grift for his mill, except what he caufed to come for his own ufe, near twenty miles on each fide of his own refidence. My Good-fir Satchels told me, that he was with Walter, called the good Lord of Buckcleugh, after he came from the fchools, and Robert of Thirlfton, after Sir Robert, they being come from the college of St Andrews, where they had been at learning, by reafon King James the VI. was of that univerfity, my Lord and Sir Robert being of the king's age, in the year one thoufand five hundred and fixty-fix, was defirous to pafs their time there; and, at their return, the Lord Buckcleugh being ready to go to his travels, was curious to fee thofe tomb-ftones

of

of his anceſtors, which was in that kirk, in the Forreſt of Rankleburn; the moſt part of the wall was
ſtanding then, and the font-ſtone within the kirk,
and a croſs before the kirk-door; the rubbiſh
and earth being caſten out, and the ſtones clean
ſwept, the Lord, and many of his friends came
to ſee them, where they did diſcern one ſtone,
which had the ancient coat of arms on it; that
is to ſay, two creſts, and a mulet born on a
counter-ſcarf, with a hunting-horn in the field,
ſupported with a hart of grace and a hart of
leice, alias a hound, and a buck, and a buck's
head torn from the creſt, which only ſeem to
be from hunters and Forreſters. The other ſtones
had drawn upon them like unto a hand and
ſword, and others of them had a ſword and a
lance all along the ſtone; Robert Scot ſaid, that
he believed, that it was four hundred years ſince
the laſt of theſe ſtones had been laid, and it was
near an hundred year ſince that time; I judge
the Lord Buckcleugh was about twenty one, or
twenty two years at that time, ſo it muſt needs
be near to an hundred years ſince.

The lands of Buckcleugh they did poſſeſs,
Three hundred years ere they had writ or wax;
And ſince that time that they a right did rear,
‘ It's ſaid to be from king Robert the third, call'd
    John Fern-year.

Now follows the feveral Places of Refidence of
the FAMILY of BUCKCLEUGH.

NOW my jocking mufe affift my rhyme com-
pleat,
I'm drown'd in profe fince thou lay down to fleep;
Thy journey's long, and fo thou muft not ftay,
'We'll take fome part of Tweeddale in our way:
The barrony of Eward was Buckcleugh's fhare,
And yet they are fuperiour,
Over-Eward, and Nether-Eward was in the barrony,
With Kirk-Eward, Lady-Eward, and Lock-Eward,
all three;
Thefe towns moft fweet furround a pleafant hill,
And Scotftoun-hall doth join unto them ftill.
It was call'd Scotftoun-hall when Buckcleugh in it
did dwell,
Unto this time it is call'd Scotftoun ftill:
It was in Kirk-Eward parifh then,
But now it's in the parifh of Lintoun;
There is three towers in it was mounted high,
And each of them had their own entry;
A fally-door did enter on,
Which ferv'd all three, and no man kend.
When Buckcleugh at Scots-hall kept his houfe,
Then Peebles-church was his burial-place,
In the crofs-kirk there has buried been
Of the lairds of Buckcleugh, either fix or feven;
There can none fay but it's two hundred year
Since any of them was buried there;
The Earls of Hamilton and Douglas,
To brave Buckcleugh fhew'd great kindnefs,

Their

Their kindnefs with him did prevail,
That he muft live near them in Clidfdale.
Scots-hall he left ftanding alone,
And went to live at Mordiftoun;
And there a brave houfe he did rear,
Which to this time it doth appear;
Several ages after, he did thefe lands excamb,
With Inglis that was the laird of Brankfome;
And fince that time I can mak't appear,
It's near two hundred and fifty year.
That family they ftill were valiant men,
No baron was better ferv'd in Britain.
The barons of Buckcleugh they kept at their call,
Four and twenty gentlemen in their hall;
All being of his name and kin,
Each two had a fervant to wait on them;
Before fupper and dinner moft renown'd,
The bells did ring and the trumpets found;
And more than that I do confefs,
They kept four and twenty penfioners;
Think not I lie, nor do me blame,
For the penfioners I can all name;
There's men alive elder than I,
They know if I fpeak truth or lie;
Ev'ry penfioner a room * did gain,
For fervice done and to be done.
Thus I'll let the reader underftand,
The name of both the men and land,
Which they poffefs'd, it is of truth,
Both from the lairds and lords of Buccleugh.

---

* By a Room is here meant a piece of Ground, or Farm, fufficient to
accommodate and maintain a family; many of thefe Rooms were very
extenfive.

But

But now, my mufe, I'll give it in thy choofe,
' Stay or go fleep, for I muft write in profe.

Now follows the Gentlemens Names who were
Penfioners to the HOUSE of BUCKCLEUGH,
with the LANDS they poffeffed for their fervice.

WALTER SCOT of North-houfe, the firft
gentleman defcended from the family, in a
former age Robert Scot of Allanmouth; David
Scot of Stobifcot, brother to Sir Walter Scot of
Gaudilands; David Scot of Raes-know, one of
the houfe of Allan-haugh; Robert Scot of Clack,
the lands of Fennick for his fervice; William Scot
in Hawick, called William in the Mott *, brother
to Walter Scot of Hardin, poffeffed thefe lands
without the Weft-port for his fervice; John Scot
of Monks-tower, brother to old William Scot of
Altoun; Robert Scot of Eafter-Groundifton, brother-fon to Robert Scot of Headfhaw; James Scot
of Altoun-Crofts, Raes-know, and Allanmouth,

* This Mott, an artificial mount of earth, raifed without the Weft-
port of Hawick, and upon the lands given to the above William Scot, is in
the form of a fugar-loaf, rifing gradually and beautifully to the height
of 52 feet; its circumference at bottom is about 313 feet, and about 126
at top, where it is quite fmooth and plain. Various are the reafons that
the common people have affigned for its being raifed; but there is no
doubt that it, like others of its kind in Scotland, was formed for the purpofe of adminiftering juftice, which in old times was always done in the
open air, and in prefence of all who chofe to attend. It is pretty certain too, that moft of thefe artificial mounts were occupied by the
Druids, as places of worfhip.

were

were all of the family of Allanhaugh; Thomas
Scot in Wester-Groundiston, brother to William
Scot of Whitehaugh, defcended of the ancient family of Buckcleugh; John Scot in Drinkfton, defcended of the ancient family of Robertoun; William Scot in Lees, alias Millma, called William
Scot of Catflac-know, defcended from the ancient
family of Dryhope; Robert Scot in Clarilaw, defcended from the ancient houfe of Haffenden;
William Scot of Totchahaugh, from the forefaid
family of Bortoheugh; Andrew Scot of Totcha-
hill, from the family of Robertoun; John Scot in
Stowflce; ——— Scot of Whames, defcended
from the North-houfe; ——— Scot of Caftlehill,
was of that kind; Walter Scot of Chappel-hill,
he was half-brother to the laird of Chifholm; Robert Scot of Howford had the lands of Cowd-
houfe for his fervice; Robert Scot of Satchels
had Southinrig for his fervice; Robert Scot of
Langup had the lands of Outter-Huntly for his
fervice, for feveral ages; there was one William
Scot, commonly called Cut at the Black, he had
the lands of Nether-Delorain for his fervice; Walter Gladftanes had Whitlaw. Thefe twenty-four
were all of the name of Scot, except Walter
Gladftanes of Whitlaw, who was nearly related to
my lord; this William Scot of Delorain, commonly called Cut at the Black, he was a brother
of the ancient houfe of Haining, which houfe of
Haining is defcended from the ancient houfe of
Haffenden; and from the forefaid William Scot
of Delorain fprung the family of Scotftorbet and
Elie,

Elie, now called Ardrofs, their original being from
Sir Alexander Scot of Haffenden ; that valiant
knight was killed with his prince, King James the
IV. at Flowden-field. Now I come to Sir Walter
Scot of Buccleugh, who was grand-father to Walter the good Lord of Buccleugh. Thefe twenty-
three penfioners, all of his own name of Scot, and
Walter Gladftanes of Whitlaw, a near coufin of
my lord's, as aforefaid, they were ready on all occafions, when his honour pleafed to caufe adver-
tife them. It was known to many in the country
better than it is to me, that the rents of thefe lands,
which the lairds and lords of Buckcleugh did freely beftow upon their friends, will amount to above
twelve or fourteen thoufand merks a-year : Thus
I have thought good to let the reader fee the be-
nefit which the younger brethren of the name had
by their chief, when he was but a Baron and
Knight, they were efteemed with more refpect
than they have been fince ; Sir William Scot of
Branxholm, who never furvived to be laird or
lord of Buccleugh, gave his lady, dame Margaret Douglas, after him countefs of Bothwell, a-
bove two and twenty thoufand merks a year of
jointure : This, with the penfioner's revenues off
the eftate, was near thirty-fix thoufand merks a-
year, which his fon Lord Walter, and his fon Earl
Walter did truly pay all their times the conjunct
fee.

Now,

Now, left you fhould think that I flatter, or am a
liar, I will nominate the lands and where they
lie, for the juftification of myfelf.

AWAKE, awake, my mufe, and me aver,
  ' To give a juft account of that jointure.
To the Piel and Hathern I will repair,
To Analfhope and Glengeber,
To Whitup and to Black-grain,
To Commonfide and Milfanton-hill,
And Eilridge is left all alone,
Except fome town-lands in Lanton.
' Now, my mufe, to the eaft country go we,
And talk of Eckfoord's barony,
Which barony fhe none did mifs,
But all into her jointure was,
In cumulo I do declare,
'Tis above twenty thoufand merks a year;
It was a worthy conjunct fee,
For a Knight to give to his lady;
That worthy houfe, when they were but gentry,
Exceeded far fome of nobility.
  O curfed Helena that the Trojans did confound,
And laid Troy's pleafant walls flat on the ground,
Her daughter had not match'd with Priamus' race,
But her mother's perfuafion made her him embrace.
  Thirty lairds and lords 'tis faid hath been,
All of Buckcleugh, yet it is uncertain;
But I believe it may be true,
I've feen four myfelf, and that I'll avow;
The nine laft generations I declare,
Both whom they married, and who they were.
At Sir Arthur Scot we begin,
In's time he was the king's warden,

H　　　　　　　　　　　　　　A

A valiant fp'rit for chivalry,
Married lord Sommervel's daughter of Cowdalie;
Sir Walter his fon did him fucceed,
Whom the borders both did fear and dread,
He was ftill forty men whene'er he rade,
He married with Douglas of Drumlanrig;
Their procreation remains unto this time,
The laft honourable fecond brother, that of that
     family came,
From that marriage Robert of Allan-haugh fprung,
'Tis near two hundred years agone,
And fince that time 'tis known to be of truth,
There was ne'er a lawful brother married from
     Buckcleugh;
The more we may repent, and figh and groan,
That they're fo Phœnix like, ftill but one.
   Sir William Scot was Sir Walter's eldeft fon,
And in his heritage he did fucceed to him,
A valiant knight, and of much renown,
He married with the honourable houfe of Hume;
His fon Sir Walter, that durft have fhown his face,
To him that was as ftout as Hercules,
He was inclin'd to blood, as was rehearft,
He was married to Ker of Farniehirft,
' To Venus her fifter, he married again,
' A beautiful creature dame Janet Beaton;
Sir William Scot of Brankfome called White-cloak,
He was fon to Buckcleugh, call'd wicked Wat,
As fortune fmil'd or frown'd,
Content that worthy was,
' He married a fifter of the houfe of Angus,
The good Lord Walter was Sir William's fon,
The better in Tiviotdale fhall never come,

                                    For

For valour, wifdom, friendfhip, love, and truth,
' He married Ker a fifter of Roxburgh;
Earl Walter was Lord Walter's fon,
A Mars for valour, wifdom, and renown,
His courage durft a Lion fear,
' His frowns would terrifi'd a Bear,
He married a fifter of Errol;
Earl Francis his father, Earl Walter, did fucceed,
' Into his Earldom, but not to his head;
Yet he wanted neither hand, head, nor heart,
But could not act like to his father's part;
His father's acts were all military,
And he was much inclin'd to ftudy;
His father fcorn'd to fuffer a ftain,
Neither of himfelf, nor of his name;
With the houfe of Rothes married he,
An equal match by antiquitie;
She was but the relict of fuch a one,
The fon of a ftart-up foldier new come home.
I have been through Scotland, Holland, and Sweden,
Yet ne'er heard of a gentleman in all his kin,
Except one Switzer, which did verifie,
' He was Bacchus' nevoy, the uncle of Brandy;
That worthy Earl was foon by death affail'd,
'Gainft whom no mortal ever yet prevail'd.
He had no heirs-male, but daughters left behind,
For to enjoy his great Earldom and lands;
Thefe infants fweet left to their guardians to keep,
Their tutors oft fuffered controul,
Their mother was fo impudent,
That fhe muft always have her intent;
The eldeft lady, I confefs, fhe was not able for a man,
With Earl Tarras fhe did wed, it was by perfua-
    fion of her dame;

Alas,

Alas, fhe liv'd not very long;
'There was no procreation them between;
I wifh to God there had been a fon,
It had been better for all poor friends;
The Countefs' fifter did her fucceed.
Then her mother to London by coach did hie,
And fearch't her a hufband beyond the fea.
A pretty youth and of high-birth,
By the name of Graves that boy did pafs;
One Mr Rofs his pedagogue was,
In France, in Holland, and in Flanders,
When the truth was known, and the lad fetcht home,
King Charles the II.'s baftard he prov'd to be,
'And I believe his maiden-head, he begat him
       young on Mrs Barly,
A pretty lady, I have her feen,'
And very gallant in her time;
Sir Thomas Barly was her fire,
A knight that dwelt in Devonfhire,
And after the reftoration,
When Charles the II. came to his home,
The Weyms Countefs, and her daughter young,
At London ftay'd, and the youth fetch'd home,
James Scot he was call'd all along,
Which did continue certain months,
And then to Windfor did return,
Where he was made Duke of Monmouth;
King Edward's badge he got, the order of the garter,
Perform'd with great folemnity, and then to Lon-
      don did repair,
His nuptial day did then draw near.
To Charing crofs he did refort,
The King and Duke royal did come there;
And moft nobles of the court;

A

A nroft proper man he in time became,
As in any princes court was feen,
Ten thoufand hearts they may lament,
That ever he fhould a rebel been ;
A rebel he was in his time,
And did the nation much perplex ;
At his invafion he was tane,
And his head cut off with an ax.

In England now the Dutchefs dwells,
Which to her friends is a curfed fate,
For if they famifh, ftarve, or die,
They cannot have a groat from that eftate.
The times of old are quite forgot,
How inferior friends had ftill relief,
And how the worthieft of the name
Engag'd themfelves to hold up their chief,
And in requital of their love,
His honour took of them fuch pains,
That they ne'er went unto the law
'Gainft one another at any time ;
In whofe cafe or caufe foever it was,
Debts, riots, or poffeffions,
Their chief he was immediate judge,—
The lawyers got nought of them.

Times have been very troublefome,
Since thefe rebellions firft began,
Which was then but forty-eight years agone,
And then our chief he was but young,
In the five and twentieth year of's age,
In the year of grace fifty and two,
He rendered up his ftewardfhip,
And had no iffue but females two ;
And as Dalila with Sampfon dealt,
When fhe cry'd the Philiftines are thee upon,

Such

Such cruel defpight, ftrife, and debate,
Remain into fome bad women;
She's like a Gardo countenanc'd like Bendo,
Cunning as Nilo peeping through a window,
Which put the wand'ring Jew in fuch amazement,
Seeing fuch a face look through the cafement;
When Lora a bull long nourifhed in Cocitus,
With fulphor horns fent by the emperor 'Titus,
Afked a ftegmatick peribeftan queftion,
If Alexander ever lived phyfician;
When Helen was for Priamus' fon a mate,
From Greece by Paris and his band,
Which caus'd the Greeks the Trojans minds abate:
Some curs'd the boys, and other fome them ban'd:
The ftrumpet Queen, which brought the burning
        brand,
That Helen fir'd, and wrak'd old Priamus race;
And on their names long living fhame did brand
For head-ftrong lufts run an unbounded race;
This beauteous piece whofe feature radiant blaze
Made Mænelaus horn mad war to wage,
And fet all Troy in a combuftious bleeze,
Whofe ten years triumphs fcarce was worth their
        wage,
For all their conquefts, and their battering rams,
' Their leaders moft return'd with heads like rams;
Lo thus the burden of adult'rous guilt,
A fhowering vengeance Troy, and Trojans faw,
No age, nor fect, no beauty, gold nor guilt,
Withftood foretold Caffandra's fecret fall;
She often faid, falfe Helen's beauteous blaft
Should be the caufe, this mighty Grecian's power,
Their names and fames with infamy fhould blaft,
                                                And

And how the gods on them would vengeance pour;
But poor Caſſandra propheſied in vain,
The clamorous crys were to the ſenſleſs rocks,
The youths of Troy in mirry ſcornful vein,
Securely ſleeps, while luſt the cradle rocks,
Till bloody burning indignations come,
And all their mirth with mourning overcome;
Yet great's the glory in the noble mind,
Where life and death are equal in reſpect,
If fates be good or bad, unkind or kind,
Not proud in freedom, nor in thral deject,
With courage ſcorning fortune's worſt effect,
In ſpitting in foul Envy's cankered face,
True honour thus doth baſer thoughts ſubject,
Eſteeming life a ſlave, that ſerves diſgrace;
Foul abject thoughts become the mind that's baſe,
That deems there is no better life than this,
Or after death doth fear a worſer place,
Where guilt is paid, the guardian of a miſs;
But let ſwoln envy ſwell until ſhe burſt.
The noble mind defys her, do her worſt;
The vulgar ſort, with open port,
Said, the Scot had much renown,
That their heiretrix was intermixt,
With a baſtard of the crown.
King James the Fifth his baſtard ſon
Was of as much regard,
He married Buckcleugh's relect,
He being but a laird.
The baſtard got into Scotland
Was never of ſuch renown,
To proſper as the Engliſh do,
They oft uſurp their crown.

King

King Arthur of the round table,
Begotten was in adultery;
And so was both king Edleston,
And William of Normandie,
But Scotland's loyal nobility
Is of a more rare degree,
Than suffer any bastard seed
To claim sovereignety.
Since the first Fergus began,
To king James the Seventh,
We have had none but twain,
Of bastards that usurp'd the crown,
And short while they did reign:
Gillis the tyrant he was one,
King Evanus the First's bastard son,
Codallus of Galloway, cut him off
In the second year of's reign;
Duncan the Second usurped the crown,
Malcolm the Third's bastard son,
But from an usurper he did it gain,
Which was from wicked Donald the Seventh.
Mackpender then of Merns the Thane,
An Earl of high renown,
He brought king Duncan to his end,
Nine months after he was crown'd.
    The bastard kings of Scotland then
Had but small prosperity,
And for the future I hope none,
In Scotland shall ever be;
Then Edgar, the just and lawful king,
Upon his throne was set,
And anointed of Dunkeld's bishop,
Whose name was Mr John Scot.

Of baſtards I will ſpeak no more,
Since I declar'd the truth;
My purpoſe now is to return,
And ſpeak of bold Buckcleugh.
That worthy valiant ſon of Mars,
That moſt illuſtrious one,
The United Provinces him ſhould blaze,
To ages that's to come.
The year and time I muſt exprime,
That from Holland came he,
The ſixteen hundred and thirty-three,
At London he did die;
In November month, to ſpeak the truth,
It was our woeful fate;
To the Bier many friends did come,
To ſee him lie in ſtate;
The nobles of the court repair'd,
Clad in their ſable weed,
And countrymen in flocks came in,
To ſee's corps when he was dead;
Patrick Scot, then of Thirlſtone,
A worthy gentleman,
He took the care of all affairs,
Caus'd his corps to be embalm'd;
All being done that wit of man
Could do or underſtand,
Then a ſhip he fraughted on the Thames,
To bring him to Scotland.
The ſhip did fall the river down,
And Greenwich did obey;
Then unto Graveſend they did come,
And two days there did ſtay;
When wind and tide they both apply'd,
And hois'd their ſails on hie,

I

Thirlſtone

Thirlftone came aboard himfelf,
Ere they reach'd Tilburie;
From once they paft by the Lands-end,
The ftorm did rife fo hie,
For three months time they liv'd in pain,
Sore toil'd upon the fea;
They were almoft funk, yet fav'd the fhip at laft,
Their fails into the fhallow feas were caft,
Yet anchor'd fafely, and did remain,
Whilft they did put to fea again:
Then 'mongft their old acquintance, ftorms and
    flaws,
Each moment near to death's devouring jaws,
The weary day they paft through many fears,
Landed at laft, quite funk o'er head and ears,
All famifh'd, ftarv'd, like filly rats all drown'd;
From fuccour far they left their fhip on ground,
Caft out their water, whilft they poorly drapt,
' And up and down to dry themfelves they hapt.
Thus they their weary pilgrimage did wear,
Expecting for the weather calm and clear:
Then madly, yet ftudy out to fea they thruft,
'Gainft winds and ftorms fo hie,
By Prignal rocks which hidden ly,
Ten miles within the fea, fome wet, fome dry,
There they fufpected danger moft of all,
If they upon thefe ragged rocks fhould fall:
But Sol, that old continual traveller,
From Titan can mount up his flaming car.
The weather kept his courfe with fire, hail, and rage,
Without appearance that it would e'er afwage;
Whilft they did pafs thefe hills, dales, and downs,
Every moment they looked to be drown'd,

                                        The

The wind ſtill blowing and the ſea ſo hie,
As if the lofty waves would kiſs the ſkie,
That many times they wiſh'd with all their hearts,
Their ſhip were ſunk, and they in landwart carts,
Or any part to keep them ſafe and dry,
The water raged ſo outrageouſly;
For it is ſaid ſince memory of man,
Or ſince winds and ſeas to ebb and flow began,
No man can mind ſuch ſtormy weather,
And continual rage ſo long together;
Thirteen long weeks that many thought,
The wind blew ſouth and ſouth-weſt,
And rais'd the ſea each wave above another,
Of fair and calm weather not an hour together,
And whether they did go by Sun or Moon,
Either by midnight or by noon;
The ſun did riſe with moſt ſuſpicious face,
Of foul forbidding weather purple red,
His radiant tincture eaſt-north-eaſt were ſpread;
In Norway by Slewgates ancient caſtle,
Againſt ragged rocks and waves they tug'd,
The moon and ſtars were covered under cloud;
By Rubnie and by Rubnie-marſh,
The tide againſt them, and the wind was harſh;
'Twixt Eolus and Neptune there was ſuch ſtrife,
That men ne'er ſaw ſuch weather in their life,
' Toſt and retoſt, retoſt and toſt again,
With a rumbling and tumbling on the rowling main;
The boiſt'rous breaking billows of the curl'd locks,
Did impetuouſly beat againſt the rocks;
The wind, which like a horſe whoſe wind is broke,
Blew thick and ſhort, that they were almoſt choak'd,
As it outrageouſly the billows heaves,
The guſt like duſt blown in the brimiſh waves;

And

And thus the wind and seas these boist'rous gods,
Fell by the ears, stark mad at furious odds;
Their stalwart ships turmoil'd 'twixt shoars and seas,
Aloft, or low, as storms and floods did please;
Sometimes upon a foaming mountain top,
Whose height did seem the heav'n to under-prop;
Then straight to such prophanity they fell,
As if they div'd into the depths of hell;
The clouds, like ripe apostoms, burst and shower'd,
Their mat'ry, watry substance head-long pour'd;
Yet though all things were mutable and fickle,
‘ They all agreed to sauce them in a pickle;
Of water fresh and salt from seas and sky,
Which with our sweat join'd in triplicity,
Bright Phœbus hid his golden head with fear,
Not daring to behold the dangers there;
Whilst in that strait and exigent they stand,
They sea and wish to land, yet durst not land,
Like rowling hills the billows beat and roar,
Against the melancholy benchy shore;
That if they landed, neither strength nor wit,
Could save their ship from being sunk or split
To keep the sea straight puffing Æolus breath,
Did threaten still to blow them unto death,
The waves amain oft boarded them,
Whilst they almost six hours did there remain;
On every side with danger and distress,
Resolv'd to run a shore at Dungeonness;
There stood some thirteen cottages together,
To shelter poor fishermen from wind and weather;
And there some people were, as they supposed,
As though the doors and windows were all closed;
They near the land, into the sea soon leapt,
To see what people there these houses kept;

They.

They knockt and call'd at each, from houfe to houfe,
But found no mankind-form, cat, rat, nor moufe;
Thefe news, all fad and comfortlefs and cold,
Amongft the crew it prefently was told,
Affuring them, the beft way they did think,
Was to leave the fhip, whether fhe fplit or fink:
Refolved thus, they altogether pleafe
To put her head to fhore, and her ftern to feas;
They leaping over-board amidft the fea,
Almoft defperate whether to live or die;
Then from top to toe they ftrend,
Pluckt off their fhirts, and then them wring'd,
Till fun and wind their want fupply'd,
And made both outfide and infide dry'd:
Two miles from thence, a filly town their ftood,
To which they went to bring fome food:
The town did fhew their pity, but for what?
They made them pay triple for what they gat;
But what they got Thirlftone ftood not for to pay
      double;
But thefe peafants made him to pay twice triple;
Becaufe thefe harbours where their fhip rode ftill,
Belong'd to men which in that town did dwell:
At Thirlftone's requeft they did fend a man,
To poffefs the crew in that hofpitable den,
With a brazen kettle, and a wooden difh,
To ferve their need, and drefs their flefh and fifh:
Then from the flefhers they brought lamb and fheep,
Ale from the Oftler-houfe, and befoms for to fweep;
Their cottage for want of ufage was moifty,
Myrifh, fluggifh, and dufty;
‘ There twenty days they did roaft, boil, and broil,
‘ And toil, and moil, and keep a noble coil:

                For

For only they kept open houſe alone,
And he that wanted beef, might eat a ſtone:
Their grand-dame Earth with beds did all befriend
     them;
And bountifully all their lengths did lend them;
That laughing or elſe lying down did make,
Their back and ſides ſore, and their ribs to ake.
Meantime in the town Thirlſtone did remain,
His lodging was little better than them.
On Saturday the winds did ſeem to ceaſe,
And brawling ſeas began to hold their peace;
Then they like tenants beggarly and poor,
Intended to leave the key beneath the door:
But that the landlord did that ſhift prevent,
Who came in pudding time and took his rent.
Then Thirlſtone came before the ſun was peeping,
They lanch'd to ſea, and left their houſe-keeping,
When preſently they ſaw the drifting ſkies,
Grin pout and lowr, and winds and ſeas 'gain riſe,
Countrymen wiſh'd Thirlſtone go by land,
To a harbour that was near at hand;
The name of it was Freſenbered,
And there their ſhip might by report be reared:
But their council was not worth a plack,
He'd never leave the ſhip, to ride on horſes back;
Yet fortune brought them to the harbour there,
Where that their ſhip they ſomewhat did repair,
And then to ſea, with mounted ſails on hie,
They bound for Scotland, and left Norway:
There was but ſmall amendment all that time,
The weather was much in one kind.
The wind and weather plaid on each ſo wild,
As if they meant not to be reconcil'd;

                                She

She, whilſt they leapt upon theſe liquid hills,
Where Purpoiſes did ſhew their phins and gills:
Yet after that, both water, wind, and ſeas,
And a pleaſant gale blew from the north north-eaſt,
Æolus and Neptune private, and no way brief;
' By providence they did arrive at Leith.
That troubleſome, toilſome journey, to be brief,
' Fifteen weeks was between London and Leith.
To all ages it ſhould ne'er be forgot,
The pains that Patrick Scot of Thirlſtone took.
Æneas on Anchiſes he took pains enough,
' But Patrick Scot he took more of the Earl of
    Buckcleugh.
    All that men can do, when princes do command,
Is their loyalty to ſhow, and venture life and land.
I've known many on Buckcleugh's means were
    bred,
Yet one night, from home, they never lay from
    bed.

THE END OF THE FIRST PART.

SATCHELS's POST'RAL,

HUMBLY PRESENTED TO HIS

NOBLE AND WORTHY FRIENDS OF THE NAMES OF SCOT AND ELLIOT, AND OTHERS.

THE THIRD EDITION,

WITH NOTES.

HAWICK:

PRINTED BY GEO. CAW.

1786.

K

To the truely Worthy, Honourable, and Right Worſhipful Sir Frances Scot of Thirlſtone, Knight-Baronet, wiſhes Earths honour and Heaven's happineſs.

THIS book, good Sir, the iſſue of my brain,
    Though far unworthy of your worthy view,
In hope ye gently it will entertain,
Yet I in duty offer it to you;
Although the method and the phraſe be plain,
Not art, like writ, as to the ſtile is due,
And truth I know your favour will obtain:
The many favours I have had from you
Hath forc'd me thus to ſhow my thankful mind,
And of all faults I know no vice ſo bad,
And hateful as ungratefully inclin'd;
A thankful heart is all a poor man's wealth,
Which with this book I give your worthy ſelf:
I humbly crave your worthineſs excuſe,
This boldneſs of my poor unlearned muſe,
That hath preſum'd ſo high a pitch to fly,
In praiſe of virtue and gentility:
I know this taſk's moſt fit for learned men,
For Homer, Ovid, or for Virgil's pen;
Theſe lines I have preſum'd to dite,
It's known to your Honour I could never write.

Your moſt obedient ſervant,

WALTER SCOT of Satchels,

SATCHELS's POST'RAL,

HUMBLY PRESENTED TO

HIS NOBLE AND WORTHY FRIENDS

OF THE

NAMES OF SCOT AND ELLIOT.

WHEN reftlefs Phœbus feem'd himfelf to reft,
His flaming car defcending to the weft,
And high Spyro obfcur'd his twinkling light;
Then in a fable mantle Madam Night,
Took of the world the fole command and keep,
Charging the eyes of mortals faft afleep:
She fends dull Morphæus forth; and fummons both,
The Ledean Potentates of fleep and flouth,
Who unto every one good reft imparts,
Save lovers guilty minds, and careful hearts;
The ftealing hours crept on with fleeping pace,
When mafked mid-night fhew'd her ebon'd face,
When hags and furies, witches, faries, elves,
Ghofts, fp'rits and goblins do feperate themfelves;
When fond imaginary dreams do reign,
In formlefs forms, in mens molefted brain;
An unaccuftom'd dream came in my head,—
I thought, as it were near by a river fide,
Within a pleafant grove I did abide,
That all the feather'd birds that fweem and fly,
Betwixt the breeding earth and fky,

One

One at the leaft of every fcveral fort,
Did for their recreation there refort;
Then there was fuch variety of notes,
Such whirling and fuch whiftling from their throats,
The bafs, the tenor, treble and the main,
All acting various actions in one ftrain.
I thought twenty-four fhepherds did draw near,
To hear the mufic of that feath'red quire;
Thefe feather'd fidlers change their notes moft fweet,
And lull'd Apollo's daughters faft afleep;
Meantime the fhepherds tript upon the mould,
Their flocks they did remain in Cupid's fold,
And the four and twenty did appear,
In three fuadrons, like martial men of weir;
If that my memory fail me not,
They were friends and kindred of the name of Scot:
' It's my happy hap to be
' Of thefe Scots relation,
' Therefore I'll dite their pedegree
' To the eight or ninth generation.

TO fpeak the truth, no man fhall me controul,
Of worthy Garrenberry, Rennalburn and Wall,
Todrick, and Gilmans-cleugh they were in my
dream,
And good Grafs-yards, and Adam in Delorain,
William in Milfinftoun, a gentleman of note,
And worthy Gaudilands, and Wauchops Walter
Scot;
Sheills-wood and Langup alfo did appear,
And Henry Scot of Palace-hill he call'd up the rear;
Thefe

These appeared to be Scots, who in the first squad
    came;
' The second squad was Elliots, I was not so well
    acquaint with them.
The second squad that appeared all into my dream,
Was the name of Elliot, and all fine gentlemen;
I am not vers'd to know from whence they came,
But sure at first they seem'd most from Las'diftoun;
Except John Elliot, where I have had good cheer,
That dwells in Unthank, he's brother to Dunlibyre;
The rest of their pedegree, I know them not,
Except Bewly and Muckledean that's related to Scot.
    The third squad are men that's void of harms,
For they are shepherd swains train'd up from bairns;
It is their daily exercise and gain,
To tend all sort of sheep, wedder, ewe, and ram;
That name of shepherd swain came first from Greece,
As plainly doth appear, by Jason's golden fleece;
Although it be not well, I caused insert with speed,
The faillings of a fool, it is no cause of feed,
Sage wisdom should accept the will for the deed;
Had I Ovid's muse, and Virgil's vein,
And wit to use Ulysses pen,
To extoll these shepherd swains, I would incline,
From Titan's rise, according to my dream.
To John Elliot in Unthank, in a storm I came late,
But now to Henry of Hare-wood I mind for to skip,
And to his brother John, and John of Thorslee-hope,
To see William Elliot of Swinside, it is my full desire,
And good John Elliot in Unthank that's brother to
    Dunlibyre;
Walter Elliot of Erkleton, he is a man of note;
' So is Muckildean his brother, he's son to Janet Scot,
                    Robert

Robert Elliot in Diuflees, the laird of Clacks his Frier,
And good William Elliot of Bewly, he drives up
      the rear;
'The rear's the fecond place, if foldiers be but ftout,
'He is fure to have the van, if the word be face about;
This was the fecond fquad appeared into my dream.
    This is the third confciencious fquad,
My author doth me affure,
Although they be but fhepherd fwains,
They do relieve the poor;
As for John Grieve in Garwold,
He keeps both board and bed,
So doth James Grieve in Lennup,
And the Grieves on Commonfide:
And it is true, John Robertfon,
Is a comrade good enough,
And for houfe-keeping he excels,
He dwells in Cauterfcleugh;
Wheat-bread, falt-beef, mutton, and old cheefe,
I riding by, he did my hunger eafe,
With capon, and lamb, brandy and good ale,
He feafted me in May, as I had been an Earl:
George Curror in Hartwoodmyers,
He is a religious man;
So is Michael Andifon in Analfhope,
And his brother John in Thirlftone;
John Tod that dwells in Tufhilaw
Can many fheep afford;
And Thomas Anderfon is not fmall,
That dwells in the Howfoord.
Unto my dream thefe were the men,
Which did appear to me,
They were four and twenty at the firft,
But fince I've added three.
                Dedicated

Dedicated to the Right Honourable

WALTER EARL OF TARRAS.

My Lord,

THE lives and deaths of knights, lords and earls,
  This little book unto your Honour tells,
Protection and acceptance if you give,
It shall, as shall yourself, for ever live;
Of all the wonders this vile world includes,
I muse how flatt'ry such high favour gains,
How adulation cunningly deludes,
Both high and low from sceptre to the swain,
But if thou by flatt'ry couldst obtain,
More than the most that is possest by men,
Thou couldst not tune thy tongue to falshood strain,
Yet with the best can use both tongue and pen,
Thy secret learning can both scan and ken,
The hidden things of nature and of art,
It's thou hast rais'd me from oblivion's den,
And made my muse from obscure sleep to start;
And to your honour's censure I commit,
The first born issue of my worthless wit,
Fresh-water soldiers fail in shallow streams,
'And Leithwind captains venture not their lives,
A brain disturb'd brings forth idle dreams,
And gilded sheaths have seldom golden knives,
And painted faces none but fools bewitch,
My muse is plain, but witty, fair, and rich:
When thou didst first to Aganipa float,
Without thy knowledge as I surely think,
Where grace and nature filling up thy fountain,
My muse came flowing from Parnassus' mountain;

L   So

So long may fhe flow as it to thee is fit,
The boundlefs ocean of a Chriftian wit;
For wit, reafon, grace, religion, nature, zeal,
Wrought altogether in thy working brain,
And to thy work did fet this certain feal,
Pure is the colour that will take no ftain.
My Lord, although I do tranfgrefs,
You know that I did never yet profefs,
Until this time in print to be a poet,
And now, to exercife my wit, I fhow it;
View but the intrals of this little book,
And you will fay that I fome pains have took,
Pains mix'd with pleafure, pleafure join'd with pain,
Produc'd this iffue of my lab'ring brain.
My dear Lord, to you I owe a countlefs debt,
Which though I ever pay, will ne'er be pay'd.
'Tis not bafe coin, fubject to canker's fret,
If fo in time my debt might be defray'd;
But this my debt I would have all men know,
Is love, the more I pay the more I owe;
Wit, learning, honefty, and all good parts,
Hath fo poffefs'd thy body and thy mind,
That covetoufly thou fteals away mens hearts,
Yet 'gainft thy fhaft there's never one repay'd:
My heart that is my greateft worldly pelf,
Shall ever be for thee as for myfelf;
Thou that in idle adulating words,
Canft never pleafe the humours of thefe days,
That greateft works with fmalleft fpeech afford,
Whofe wit the rules of wifdom's love obeys;
In few words then, I wifh that thou mayft be,
As well belov'd of all men as of me.
To virtue and to honour once in Rome,
Two ftately temples there erected was,

Where

Where none might into honour's temple come,
But firſt through virtues temple they muſt paſs;
Which was an emblem and an document,
That men by virtue muſt true honour win;
And how that honour ſhall be permanent,
Which only did from virtue firſt begin.
Could envy die if honour were deceas'd,
She could not live for honour's envy's food,
She iives by ſucking of the noble blood,
And ſcales the lofty top of fames high creſt,
Baſe thoughts compacted in the object's breaſt,
The meagure monſter doth neither harm nor good,
But like the wain, or wax, or ebb, or flood,
She ſhuns as what her age doth moſt detaſte,
Where heaven bred honour in the noble mind,
From out the cavern of the breaſt proceeds,
Their hell-born envy ſhews her helliſh kind,
And vulture-like upon the actions feed;
But here's the odds, that honour's tree ſhall grow
When envy's rotten ſtump ſhall burn in low.

   My Lord, I know your honour knows,
That I muſt ſpeak the truth:
John Scot he was a natural ſon,
To Walter Earl of Buckcleugh,
Begot on Madam Drummond,
A noble lady by birth,
By kindred couſin-german
To the right honourable Earl of Perth:
He promiſed her wedlock, and prov'd unto her ſo,
ʿAs Prince Æneas did to the Carthage Queen Dido;
But yet let their ſucceſſion
Live ſtill in memory
He was a worthy valiant ſquire,
ʿJohn Scot of Gorinberry;

At

At the beauty of all the nine,
He hit the mark,
And married Sir John Liddle's daughter,
' Knight Baron and Baronet;
And betwixt thefe worthy couple, procreat there be,
This prefent Francis Scot, the good laird of Gor-
        rinberry,
He hath gain'd the conftant and true Penelope,
He's married to Sir John Wauchop's daughter,
That old baron of Niddrie,
Whofe names and fames, birth and antiquity,
Surpaffes many ladies of fome nobility;
I have declar'd the family,
Of the worthy lairds of Gorinberry,
And hopes his honour thinks no fhame,
For to be call'd a fhepherd fwain.

  Our father Adam's fecond fon, a prince
As great as any man begotten fince,
Yet in his function he a fhepherd was,
And fo his mortal pilgrimage did pafs;
And in the facred text it is compil'd,
That he that's father of the faithful ftil'd,
Did as a fhepherd live upon th' increafe
Of fheep on earth, until his days did ceafe;
And in thefe days it was apparent then,
' Abel and Abram both were noblemen:
The one obtain'd his title righteoufly,
For his unfeigned ferving the Moft High;
He firft did offer fheep, which on record
Was facrifice accepted of the Lord,
Since patriarchs were fhepherds
In Arcadia, and Greece,

                                I wifh

I wish the wool in Etherstone-sheils,
May grow like Jason's fleece.

Walter Scot of Highchester, a man of fine accomplishments,
and in great favour with king Charles II. was by the king
created Earl of Tarras for life; but the honours did not
descend to his posterity. He married first Mary, countess
of Buckcleugh; but she died without issue. He married
2dly, Helen, eldest daughter of Thomas Hepburn of Hum-
bie, Esq; by whom he had three sons and three daughters.
Walter Scott Esq; second son of Walter Earl Tarras, upon the death of his nephew, John Scott of Harden without
male-issue, succeeded to his estate and titles, as heir-male
and of entail, in 1734. Baronage of Scotland, page 216. By
which succession the honours of Highchester or Tarras are
now sunk in the family of Harden.

ᴖᴖᴖᴖᴖᴖᴖᴖᴖᴖᴖᴖᴖᴖᴖᴖᴖᴖᴖᴖ

Dedicated to the very Honourable, and Right Worshipful

SIR FRANCIS SCOT OF THIRLSTONE.

SIR, my weak collections out hath took,
'The sum and pith of sundry chronicle books;
For pardon and protection I intreat,
The volume's little but my presumption's great.
Sir, since all memorandums of fore past ages,
Sayings, and sentences of ancient sages,
The glory of Apollo's radient chine
The supporter of the sacred sisters nine,
The Atlas that all historians do bear,
Throughout the world, here and every where;
Whoever went behind you, I would ken,
Whose worth throughout the spacious nation ring.
                                        Since

Since Rennal-burn, your worſhip's kinſman near,
He hath thoſe ſheep which golden fleeces wear,
And it may be, it is ſuch beaſt and fleece,
Which Jaſon brought from Cholkis into Greece ;
John Scot the ſquire of Newburgh-hall,
Alias of Rennal-burn as men him call,
To the firſt John Scot of Rennal-burn late,
He was the ſon and heir to his eſtate,
Who was the ſon of that Sir John Scot of worth,
The prince of poets, and knight of Newburgh,
Chaucer Glover, and Sir Thomas More,
And Sir Philip Sidney, who the laurel wore,
They never had a more poetical vein,
Than Newburgh's John, that was Mr Arthur's ſon.
And Mr Arthur was a learned man,
Son to Simon Scot of Newburgh then.
This Simon Scot's call'd Simon with the ſpear,
Tutor of Thirlſtone was both for peace and wear ;
That Simon Scot, a bold and reſolute man,
He was ſon to John Scot of Thirlſtone ;
John Scot of Thirlſtone,
My good-ſir let me knaw
He was ſon to David Scot of Howpaſlaw ;
That David Scot he did excell,
'Mongſt all hunters he bore the bell ;
He did abound for wit and ſkill ;
All his aſſociates did wear a tod tail ;
Which they eſteem moſt by their engadges,
More than French gallants do of their plumages.
David of Howpaſlaw, he was the ſon
Of the firſt Sir Walter, e'er was of that room,
He was a man of credit and renown,
He married Elliot daughter to the laird of Lariſton ;
David of Howpaſlaw, Sir Walter's ſon,

He

He married with Scot, a daughter of Robertoun;
His fon John Scot of Thirlftone a man of worth,
He married Scot, the daughter of the laird of
    Allenhaugh.
John's fon, Robert, was warden in his time,
The fight of Robert's hill he did gain;
He for his king and country did maintain the truth;
He married Scot, daughter to the laird of Buccleugh;
The firft Sir Robert Scot of Thirlftone was his fon,
He married Margaret, daughter to the laird of
    Cranfton;
Sir Robert Scot his fon, for whofe death I mourn,
He married Lyon, daughter to the mafter of King-
    horn.
His death was fad to all his near relations,
A worthy man was he,
And died without fucceffion:
Then Patrick Scot his father's-brother fon,
Took on the defignation of Thirlftone,
A very worthy courteous man was he,
He married Murray, daughter to the Laird of
    Blackbarony;
His fon Sir Francis Scot, Knight Baronet Thirlftone,
Is now married to Ker, daughter to William Earl
    of Louthian.
Of his genealogy I've faid enough,
His original it is of Buckcleugh;
Yet were it no more but fo I dare be bold,
To think this land doth many Jafon's hold;
Who never yet did pafs a dangerous wave,
Yet may with eafe its golden fleeces have.
' My little book whofo doth entertain,
' It's dedicate to none but gentlemen;
' Sometimes to old, fometimes to young,
                         ' Sometimes

' Sometimes to the father, fometimes to the fon,
' Sometimes to the great, fometimes to the fmall,
' So my book it keeps no rule at all.

The family of Thirlftone was anciently defigned of Efkdale, or
Howpafley, as appears by the genealogical account of the
family; but, upon Thirlftone being added to their poffeffions,
they thought proper to take their defignation from thefe
lands. John Scot of Thirlftone (fon and fucceffor to Robert Scot of Howpaifley, the firft that defigned himfelf of Thirlftone), was a gentleman of entire loyalty;
and for his ready fervices to his fovereign James V. was
honoured by that king, as a fpecial conceffion of his favour,
with a part of the Royal-enfign, and other fuitable figures,
to adorn his Armorial-bearing, under his majefty's hand,
and the fubfcription of Sir Thomas Erfkine of Brichen Se-
cretar, as follows.

> JAMES REX,
> "WE James by the Grace of God King of Scots, confi-
> "derand the Faith and good Servis of right traift friend,
> "John Scot of Thirlftaine, quha command to our Hoft at Sautra
> "Edge, with threefcore and ten Launciers on horfe-back, of
> "his friends and followers. And beand willing to gang with
> "us into England, when all our nobles and others refufed, he
> "was ready to flake all at our bidding; for the which caufe,
> "it is our will: And we do ftrictly command and charge our
> "Lion Herauld and his Deputis for the time beand, to give
> "and to grant to the faid John Scot, an border of Flower-de-
> "Liffes, about his Coat of Arms, fick as in our Royal-banner,
> "and alfefwae an Bundel of Launces, above his Helmet, with
> "thir words, Readdy ay Readdy; that he and all his after-
> "cummers may bruck the famen, as a pledge and taiken of
> "our good-will and kindnefs for his trew worthinefs. And
> "thir our letters feen, ye naeways failzie to do. Given at
> "Falamuire, under our hand and Privy Casket, the xxvii day
> "of July, 1542 years.

> By the King's fpecial Ordinance,
> THOMAS ARESKINE.

Sir

Sir William Scott of Thirlstone (son and successor of Sir Francis, to whom our author dedicates the foregoing epistle), married Elisabeth Napier, daughter to the lady Napier. Sir William's lady dying in 1705, and her mother in 1706, the honour of Lord Napier devolved to Francis, only son of Sir William Scott, by which the honours and estate of Thirlstone sunk in the family of Napier.

Dedicated to that worthy and compleat gentleman,

ROBERT SCOT, SECOND SON TO SIR WILLIAM SCOT OF HARDIN.

UNLEARNED Azo store of books hath bought,
   Because a learned scholar he'll be thought;
I counsell'd him that had of books such store,
To buy pipes, flutes, the viol, and bandore,
And then his music, and his learning share,
Being both alike, with either might compare;
He did both beat his brain, and try his wit,
In hopes thereby to please the multitude;
As soon may he ride a horse without a bit,
Above the moon or sun's high altitude:
Then neither flattery, nor the hope of pelf,
Hath made me write, but for to please myself:
Though sin and hell work mortals to betray,
Yet 'gainst their malice, God still arms thy way;
Thou canst behave amongst those banks and briers,
As well as he who to cedars-top aspires,
Or to the lowest shrub, or branch of broom,
That hath its breeding from earth's stumbling
   womb.

M

And

And now I talk of broom, of fhrubs and cedars,
Me thinks a world of trees, are now my leaders.
To profecute this travel made with pain,
And make comparifon betwixt trees and men;
The cedars, and the high-clouds kiffing pines,
Fœcunds, olives, and the crooked vines,
The elm, the afh, the oak, the maftie beech,
The pear, the apple, and the rough ground peach;
And many more, for it would tedious be,
To name each fruitful and unfruitful tree.
For to proceed, and fhew how men and trees,
In birth and breed, in life and death agrees.
In their beginning they have both one birth,
Both have their natural being from the earth;
Thofe that 'fcape fortune, and th' extreams of love,
Unto their longeft home by death are drove,
Where Cefars, Kefars, fubjects objects muft,
Be all alike confum'd to dirt and duft:
Death endeth all our cares, or cares increafe,
It fends us unto lafting pain, or blefs;
Where honour is with noble virtue mixt;
It like a rock ftands permanent and fixt.
The fnares of Envy, or her traps of hate,
Could never, nor fhall ever hurt that ftate.
Like adament it beats back the battery,
Of fpightful malice, and deceiving flattery.
For it with pride can never be infected,
But humbly is fupernally protected;
A fupporter, or prop I wifh Robert may be,
As Rowlin call'd Robert was to Normandy.
Robert call'd John Fern-year was in Scotland,
So was Robert Bruce his revenging powerful hand.
I wifh thee health, wealth, and renown,
Without any expectation of a crown:

This

This dedication which to your hands takes fcop,
Concerns a fhepherd from Will Scot of Langup,
Who's a prudent, wife, and civil gentleman,
As many that live in this part of the land;
Who fprung from a worthy ftock of late,
Who was named John Scot of Langup,
Who was the fon, I very well knew,
Of John Scot of Headfhaw;
And John Scot, we all do ken,
Was fon to George Scot of Sinton;
And George Scot, called How-coat,
Was fon of Sinton's youngeft Wat;
And young Wat was Walter's fon,
That was Laird of Sinton, whence Hardin fprung,
And Walter he was George's fon,
And George he was the fon of John;
For Walter and William was two brether,
His name was George that was their father.
My memory is Lord-keeper of my treafure,
And great underftanding gives true juftice meafure,
To good, to bad, to juft and to unjuft,
Invention and remembrance waits the leifure
Of memory and underftanding moft,
Hath wifdom for her fellow and her guide;
Elfe princes, peers and commons ftray afide;
For William Scot in our fouth part of Greeces,
I wifh may ne'er want fuch as Jafon's golden fleeces.

The above Robert Scott, defigned of Ilifton, upon the death
of his elder brother, Sir William, without iffue, anno 1707,
fucceeded to the eftate of Harden; but he dying alfo without iffue, anno 1710, in him ended the whole male-line of
Sir William, eldeft fon of the firft Sir William of Harden.—
Baronage of Scotland p. 216.

Dedicated to the worthy and well accomplished gentleman,

WILLIAM SCOT OF RAE-BURN.

THE juftice, mercy, and the might I fing,
  Of Heaven's juft, merciful, almighty king,
By whofe fore-knowledge all things were elected,
Whofe power hath all things made, and all projected;
Whofe mercies flood hath quencht his juftice flame,
Who is, fhall be one, and ftill the fame.
Who in the prime, when all things firft began,
Made all for man, and for himfelf made man:
Made, not begotten, or of human birth,
No fire but God, no mother but the earth,
Who ne'er knew childhood, or the fucking-teat,
But at the firft was made a man compleat;
Whofe inward foul in God-like form did fhine,
As image of the majefty divine:
Whofe fupernatural wifdom beyond nature,
'Did name each fenfible and fenfelefs creature;
And from whofe ftar-like, fand-like generation,
Sprung every kindred, kingdom, tribe and nation.
All people then one language fpoke alone,
Interpreters the world then needed none;
There lived then no learned deep grammarians,
There was no Turks, no Scythians, nor Tartarians;
Then all was one, and one was only one,
The language of the univerfal ball;
Then if a traveller had gone as far,
As from the Artick to the Antartick ftar,
If he from Boreas into Aufter went,
Or from the Orient to the Occident,
Which way fo ever he did turn or wind,
He had been fure his countryman to find;

One

O ne undred thirty winters fince the flood,
The earth one only language underftood,
Until the fon of Cufh, the fon of Cham,
A proud cloud-fcaling tower began to frame,
Trufting, that if the world again were drown'd,
He in his lofty building might reft found ;
All future floods he purpos'd to prevent,
Afpiring to Heaven's glorious battlement ;
' But high Jehovah with a puff was able,
' To make ambitions Babel but a bauble.
Thefe fhepherd fwains, I fend into your view,
Are thirty one, a very worthy crew ;
Fifteen of them are gentlemen of note,
All of the renown'd name of Scot ;
Whereof Henry Scot in Palifhil is one,
The youngeft fhepherd fwain of all the name
He's natural fon unto that bold Baron.
Sir John Scot the knight of Ancrum ;
Both wealth and wifdom his father doth embrace,
And he abounds in Jafon's golden fleece.

✤✤✤✤✤✤✤✤✤✤✤✤✤✤✤✤✤✤✤✤✤✤✤✤✤

Dedicated to the illuftrious and worthy gentleman,

THOMAS SCOT OF WHITSLADE.

MOST worthy Sir, I have with pain and la-
bour took,
To fearch fome hift'ries for this little book,
I have it all gathered from thence,
' Efpecially things of greateft confequence ;
And though the volume and the work be fmall,
Yet it does contain the fum of all ;

To

To you I give it, with a heart moft fervent,
And refts your humble and obedient fervant.
   For fhepherd fwains they have been long
The glory of their land,
The beft of men has been a fwain,
Behold brave Tamerlane ;
Then Walter Scot now of Todrick,
Since thou'rt a gentleman,
I'm fure thou'll not offended be,
To be call'd a fhepherd fwain ;
Thy father Thomas did the like,
Since he to Todrick came.
Thomas thy good-fire was a fwain,
When he from Whitflade fprung ;
Thy grandfire, brave Walter of Whitflade,
Was call'd the hawk complete,
A man of note and good report,
Yet had many flocks of fheep ;
His father Robert, thy great grandfire,
Of Stirches was defign'd,
Becaufe his father, Walter Scot,
Liv'd at Witflade in his time,
He was a worthy gentleman,
And kept a great menzie ;
There was ninety years paft o'er his head
Before that he did die.
The reft of your genealogie
I can you well declare,
They were all worthy gentlemen ;
But I will talk nae mair.
   To fpeak of Whitflade's family
Or when it did begin,
'Tis above two hundred years ago ;
It was in the fourteen hundred and eighty-feven ;
                         Walter

Walter the firft of Whitflade then,
Was Hardin's elder brother,
He married a fair comely dame,
Daughter to the laird of Riddel ;
Robert his father did fucceed,
In heritages, mains, and mill,
And married with one Rutherford,
Daughter to the Laird Hunthill ;
His fon Walter, fharp as a hawk,
For valour he did pafs,
He married with a comely dame,
Daughter to Cavers Douglas ;
His fon Sir Walter Scot, if I did forget
I fhould be much to blame,
He married with Sufanna Scot,
Daughter to the Laird of Thirlftane ;
And after her he married again,
Which I do know for truth,
Unto a very comely lafs,
Sifter to Sir John Scot of Newburgh ;
His fon Robert Scot of worthy note,
' Holland's Jean married he,
Natural daughter to Walter Lord Buckcleugh,
She was a frugal lady.
Sir Walter Scot, brother to Robert,
He married a lady fair,
Daughter to Sir Robert Stuart of Ormftoun,
' Who is brother to John Earl of Traquair ;
Thomas his brother did him fucceed,
A man of worthy fame,
A virtuous lady he did wed,
Madam Mitchel was her name.
Thomas his fon doth now remain.
The eighth laird of that part,

He's

He's married to a frugal dame,
Daughter to Sir John Hay of Park.
Thomas, the laft that of Whitflade we loft,
Was a man of good efteem,
He departed in the year of grace
Sixteen hundred and feventy-one.
Sir Walter Scot, his brother, that
At Innerkeithing was flain,
It was into the year of grace
Sixteen hundred and fifty-one ;
His brother Robert that bold baron,
It was an woeful hour,
At York's great fight he loft his life *,
In the fixteen hundred and forty-four.
Their father, brave Sir Walter Scot,
The chief of chivalry,
In the fixteen hundred and twenty-eighth year,
At Whiflade he did die.
Of Whitflade's worthy family,
I will no further dite,
For he does know affuredly,
I can neither read nor write.
Ulyffes was a happy man of men,
In that his acts were writ with Homer's pen ;
And Virgil wrote the actions of the glory,
Of brave Æneas and his wandring ftory ;
The fhepherds live, and thus they end their lives,
With good and brave and juft prerogatives.

The above Thomas Scott of Whitflade, who married Jane,
daughter to Sir J. Hay of Park, Bart. in the fhire of Galloway, had by her feven fons ; all of whom died without if-

* See Poetical Mufeum, p. 189,

fue,

sue, except the eldest, Thomas, who succeeded his father, and married a daughter of Sir J. Scott, of Ancrum, Bart. in Roxburghshire, and by her had two daughters, viz. Elizabeth and Janet;—Janet died unmarried;—and Elizabeth was married to Mr William Macdougal, brother to —— Macdougal of Mackerstoun, in Berwickshire, by whom she had issue.——Thomas was succeeded in the estate of Whitslade by his brother and male heir, John, who was never married; he sold the estate of Whitslade in, or about the year 1722, and died some few years after;—and which estate consisted, at that time, of Whitslade, Castilside, two large farms called Redfordgreens, Askirk, Askirkmill, Salanside, Bradley, &c. &c. all in Roxburghshire.——With this John (so far as we can possibly find out) ended the male line of this principal branch of the ancient family of Sinton. ——Vide Pedigree of —— Scott of Stokoe, p. 15, 16.

Dedicated to that worthy gentleman,

JOHN SCOT OF WOOL,

Brother german to Sir WILLIAM SCOT of Hardin, Elder.

MOST worthy Sir, into your hands I give,
　The sum of that which makes me so brief,
I humbly crave acceptance at your hand,
And rests your servant ever to command.
　Since I've begun, I hope to make an end,
And as I can my shepherd swains defend;
For Walter Scot of Wall,
These lines I do design:
For there are many gallants
That have shepherds been;

N　　　　　　　　　　　　Rome's

Rome's fond Romulus was bred and fed,
'Mongft fhepherds where his youthful days he led.
The Perfian Monarch Cyrus he did pafs,
His youth with fhepherds, and a fhepherd was;
Wherefore I humbly thee intreat,
' If I do call thee fhepherd, not to fret;
For I know ye are all gentlemen,
To the feventh or eighth generation:
And I will do to you that I'll not do to others,
' For I'll defcribe you both your fathers and mothers;
Becaufe erroneous liars the old family did not ken,
Call'd Hardin, this and that faid, they're not gen-
    tlemen;
Wherefore I will at William begin,
Brother german to Walter of Sinton,
Who was a man of great command,
He enjoyed all Sinton's Lordfhip,
And the Beat-up land;
He was the fon of George,
Who did enjoy the fame,
So did his father, his name was John:
George left his fecond fon, it is moft clear,
'Twixt four and five thoufand merks a year,
Into that poffeffion at that time,
I know not what charter and evidence was then:
Yet to let mifbelieving people ken,.
Thefe lands as they ly, I will defign;
Therefore William was a valiant man,
Who was the firft Laird of Hardin:
In his poffeffion he had then no lefs
Than Hardin, Totfhaw, Mebenlaw, and High-
    chefters,
With Todrick, which good fheep afford;
Wefter Effenfide, Burnfoot, and Shiellswood;
                    Thefe

Thefe were the lands I do explain,
That George of Sinton gave his fon William;
Why fhould ramping liars blaft his fame,
And fay that he was not a gentleman;
He wanted nothing of gentry,
But only the title of dignity:
The firft lady that he did gain,
Was daughter to the baron of Chifholm,
' Then in Hardin place he did fit down,
' And on her there begat one only fon;
For within fhort procefs of fwift time,
She dy'd e'er fhe came to her prime:
The laird a widower did remain,
How long a time I do not ken;
But his fon he grew up to be a man,
The firft Walter Scot of Hardin:
Then Hardin did to Riddel ride,
The old laird of Riddel being dead,
In fuit of his relict there came he,
She was a daughter of Fairnilie;
She was a fair and beauteous dame,
And at that time fhe was but young;
Her beauty others did excell,
She had one daughter to Riddel,
Brave William Scot he did her gain,
They had not been long in that room,
While the lady's daughter married the laird's fon;
Then they left the young folk in Hardin,
And the old folk in Todrick they fat down,
' And there they did two fons beget,
' Robert of Burnfoot, and George of Todrick;
And both of them prov'd ftout able men,
They were the firft cadents come of Hardin:
Now to the young folks I return,

The Laird and Lady of Hardin,
Betwixt them was procreat a fon,
Call'd William Bolt-foot of Hardin;
He did furvive to be a man,
And then to the Fairnilie he came;
And Fairnilie's daughter he did wed;
For they were related by kindred:
Betwixt them two was procreat,
The ftout and valiant Walter Scot
Of Hardin, who can never die,
But live by fame to the tenth degree:
He became both able, ftrong and ftout,
Married Philip's daughter, fquire of Dryhope,
Which was an ancient family,
And many broad lands enjoyed he;
Betwixt thefe Scots was procreat,
That much renown'd Sir William Scot,
I need not to explain his name,
Becaufe he ever lives by fame;
He was a man of port and rank,
He married Sir Gideon Murray's daughter of Eli-
      bank;
Betwixt them there was procreat,
This old Sir William that's living yet:
This old Sir William married
A fifter of the houfe of Boyd,
And there's procreat them betwixt,
Sir William Scot, now call'd youngeft,
' Becaufe his father does remain,
' Therefore he's called young Sir William;
And young Sir William married
The only daughter of Sir John Nifbet,
He late was advocate to the king,
And now is call'd Lord Dirltown:

                                  This

This genealogy is true,
And the old was as good as the new.
Now worthy Wall, I wifh thee life and health,
Hoping thou'll ne'er marry inferior to thyfelf;
Yet ambition, pomp, and hell-begotten pride,
And damn'd adulation thou will ftill deride;
The complimental flattery of kings courts,
I hope fhall ne'er be mixt amidft thy fports:
For Homer was the prime of poets ftil'd,
And worthy actions ftill he did compile;
That he did both in Arcadia and Greece,
Exftol the fhepherds with Jafon's golden fleece.

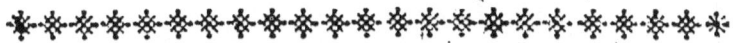

Dedicated to the Honourable and well accomplifhed gentleman,

SIR WILLIAM SCOT OF HARDIN, KNIGHT.

UNTO the profpect of your wifdom's eyes,
   I confecrate thefe filly lines,
Not that I think them worthy of your view,
But, beaufe in love my thoughts are bound to you;
I do confefs myfelf unworthy far,
To dite in fuch like cafes as they are:
Which Homer, Virgil, nor the fluent Tullic,
In fitting terms could fcarce exprefs them fully:
For Francis Scot of Gilman's-cleugh,
To you I do commend,
In hopes your worfhip ftill will be his friend,
The fon of John, the fon of Robert, call'd Truth,
Who was the fon of James,
The firft of Gilman's-cleugh,
A valiant gentleman, who well deferv'd renown,
                                                    He

He was the youngeſt ſon to John Scot of Thirlſton,
The which John Scot he did excell,
Being ſon to David with the tod's tail;
And David Scot, my author let me know,
He was ſon to Walter of Howpaſlaw;
Sir Walter he was William's ſon,
Of the worthy houſe of Buccleugh he ſprung,
The lads in Gilman's-cleugh,
In hunting did excell;
So did their father David,
That carried the tod's tail,
Who had as much delight,
In hunting of that beaſt,
As Jaſon had in Greece
To bear the golden fleece.

✳✳✳✳✳✳✳✳✳✳✳✳✳✳✳✳✳✳✳✳✳✳✳✳✳

Dedicated to the Right Honourable,

SIR JOHN SCOT OF ANCRUM, Knight.

Wiſhes mirth and happineſs be ſtill your attendants.

THE guns proclaim'd aloud on every hill,
 The joyful acclamations of the Scots people;
The which did thunder with ſo high a ſtrain,
As if great Mars they meant to entertain:
True mirth and gladneſs was on every face,
And healths run bravely round in every place;
That ſure I think the ſeventh day of July,
At the Reid-ſwair * ſhould ne'er forgotten be;

For a particular account of this memorable Battle, ſee Poetical Muſeum
(printed at Hawick 1784), p. 235.

        That

That was a day to his everlafting fame,
The valiant Laird Wat brought in the worthy
 name;
That day fhould ever be dedicate to mirth,
As if it had been a great fovereign's birth:
When valiant Wat, that worthy man,
Brought in the name of Scot, well to be feen;
It was nothing you'll fay to bring them in,
But to th' effufion of his blood
He brought them back again;
The executors and tutors, that hath been in our
 time,
The honour of the Scots did ne'er fo much pro-
 claim;
The old verfe I muft give in,
' Though men fhould fay that I am drunken,
How Wat thy good-fire, that worthy man,
To the Reid-fwair brought his troop,
The feventh day of July, the footh to fay,
At the Reid-fwair the tryft was fet;
Our wardens they did fix a day,
As they appointed, fo they met.
The Lord Buckcleugh he was but young,
Carmichael was warden in his place,
The Laird Wat, that worthy man,,
Commanded the firname with great grace:
Thy pedigree is foon defcribed,
I think I may do it well enough.
Thy father, Charles, was Laird Wat's fon,
Who was natural fon to Scot of Buckcleugh,
Their generations are formerly defcribed,
I need them not defcribe again,
Both Walter's and William's and Sir Arthur;
Unto the ninth generation;

       From

From whence fuch men may gather their relief,
That though a ram-head may be caufe of grief,
Yet nature hath a remedy found out,
They fhould have lions hearts to bear it out ;
Though I call'd thee fhepherd fwain,
Yet I deferve no blame ;
I hope that Jafon's golden fleece
With thee ftill fhall remain.

Dedicated to the right worfhipful, and very honourable, and moſt generous gentleman,

SIR WILLIAM SCOT OF HARDIN, Younger.

THE Prince of princes and the King of kings,
  Whofe eye of providence forefees all things,
To whom whatever was, or ever fhall be,
Is prefent ftill before his Majefty,
Who doth difpofe of all things as he lift,
' And grafpeth time in his eternal fift ;
He fees and knows for us what's bad or good,
And all things is by him well underftood,
Mens weak conjecture no man can arreid,
What in the eternal parliament's decreed ;
And what the Trinity concludeth there,
We muft expect it with obedience here ;
Then let not any man prefume fo far,
To fearch what the Almighty's councils are ;
But let our wills attend upon his will,
And let his will be our direction ftill :
Let not Plebeians be inquifitive,
Nor into any profound ftate bufinefs dive.

We into the thousand and sixteenth year,
Since Fergus our first king did appear,
Have many hopeful royal princes had,
Who, as heaven pleas'd to bless, were good or bad.
Fergus was the first which we had crown'd,
For learning and for wisdom high renown'd ;
Beyond the verge of Christendom's swift fame,
Did make the world admire his noble name.
A hundred and eleven we've had crown'd sincesyne,
' Whereof one of them was a queen ;
Their valour and triumphant victories
Have fill'd the world, and mounts into the skies :
As Kenneth the second, that king of victory,
And Gregorius Magnus, whose fame can never die.
Robertus Brucius, that king of high renown,
King James the Sixth, that united the three crowns;
These victorious princes govern'd well,
But more have been of the contrair strain.
Love sometimes made the gods themselves dif-
        guise,
And muffle up their mighty deities,
And virtuous princes of the gods have odds,
When princes goodness doth out-go the gods.
' I'm a foolish man, this is no work of mine,
' 'Tis an operation of the power divine.
Let God alone, for what he hath in hand,
'Tis saucy, folly and madness, to withstand
What his eternal wisdom hath decreed,
Who better knows than we do what we need.
To him let's pray for his most safe protection,
Him we implore for his most sure direction ;
Let his assistance be the seventh king James's guide,
That in the end God may be glorified.

O   ' Let

'Let us amendment in our lives exprefs,
'And let our thanks be more our fins be lefs.
Thy coufin William Scot in Milfington,
He is an worthy gentleman,
Come of a worthy family,
For he from Whitflade fprung;
Of his brother Todrick I have wrote,
And given a true relation,
Of his moft worthy pedigree,
Unto the feventh or ninth generation;
Therefore it is needlefs unto me,
To write them over again;
For if I pleafe, I could revife
'Them to the fifteenth generation.
According to my dream, he is the fhepherd fwain,
I hope Jafon's golden fleece with him fhall ftill
     remain.

*Dedicated to the very worfhipful, and much honoured generous
gentlemen,*

HUGH SCOT of GALLOWSHIELLS, and WAL-
TER SCOT in WAUCHOP.

O! For a quill of that Arabian wing,
   That's hatch't in embers of fome kindled fire,
Who to herfelf, herfelf doth iffue bring,
And, three in one, is young, and dame and fire:
O! that I could to Virgil's vein afpire,
Or Homer's verfe, the golden language Greek,
With polifh'd phrafes, I my lines would tire,
Into the deep of art my mufe fhould feek;
Meantime amongft the vulgar fhe muft throng,
Becaufe fhe hath no help from my unlearned tongue;
                                        Great

Great is the glory of the noble mind,
Where life and death are equal in refpect,
If fates be good or bad, unkind or kind;
Not proud in freedom nor in thrall dejeдt;
With courage fcorning fortune's worlt effect,
And fpitting in fond envy's cankered face,
True honour thus doth bafer thoughts dejeдt;
Efteeming life a flave that ferves difgrace,
Foul abject thoughts become the mind that's bafe,
That deems there is no better life than this,
Or after death doth fear a worfer place,
Where guilt is pay'd the guardian of a mifs;
But let fwoln envy fwell until fhe burfl,
The noble mind defies her, do her worft;
If Homer's verfe in Greek did merit praife,
If Nafo in the Latin won the bayes,
If Maro amongft the Romans did excell,
If Tofa in the Teftine tongue wrote well;
A foldier that could never lead a pen,
Shows to the eighth or ninth gereation,
Although I him enrol, and call him fhepherd fwain,
Yet hereby I approve he is a gentleman,
The fon of Adam, who was by lot,
The brother of the worthy Colonel Scot,
Who died with honour at Dumbar's fight,
In maintenance of king and country's right:
He was the fon, I know it for truth,
Of William Scot, laird of Whithaugh;
And William Scot was the eldeft fon
Of Walter Scot, ftil'd of the fame;
Walter Scot was Robert's fon,
And Robert he was Walter's fon:
The firft of Whitehaugh that from Borthwick
    fprung,

                                        That

That Wat of Whitehaugh was coufin-german
To John of Borthwick, who fafted fo long,
' Three fundry times he did perform
' To falt forty days, I do aver;
Bifhop Spotfwood, my author is he,
A profound learn'd prelate that would not lie:
When James the V. he was Scotland's King,
In the Caftle of Edinburgh he incarcer'd him,
And would not believe the country fays,
That any mortal could faft forty days;
Bear-bread and water the king allow'd for his meat,
But John Scot refus'd, and would not eat:
' When the forty days were come and gone,
' He was a great deal luftier than when he began.
Then of the king he did prefume,
To beg recommendation to the Pope of Rome,
' Where there he fafted forty days more,
' And was neither hungry, fick, nor fore;
From Rome he did haftily return,
And arrived in Britain at London;
Where Henry the eighth he got notice,
That John Scot had fafted twice forty days;
The king would not believe he could do fuch thing,
For which he commanded to incarcerate him;
Forty days expir'd, he faid he had no pain,
Than his faft had been but ten hours time:
Here Walter Scot, I'll draw near an end,
From John of Borthwick thy fathers did defcend;
He was the fon of Walter, I have faid enough,
Their original is from Buckclengh.
In the fourfcore pfalm we read,
That like a flock our God did Jofeph lead,
And ev'ry day we do confefs almoft,
That we have err'd, and ftray'd like fheep that's loft,
                                        For

For oaths and paffing words, and joining hands,
Is like affurance written in the fands,
The filly fheeps-fkin turn'd to parchment thin, ·
Shows that Jafon's golden fleece with thee remains.

ᵜᵜᵜᵜᵜᵜᵜᵜᵜᵜᵜᵜᵜᵜᵜᵜᵜᵜᵜᵜᵜ

*Dedicated to the Right Worfhipful and truely generous, my well
approved good friend,*

SIR PATRICK SCOT OF LONG-NEWTON,
APPEARANT OF ANCRUM, KNIGHT.

IT's fuch a title of preheminence then,
'To bear the name of fhepherd fwain,
That David who fo well his words did frame,
Did call our great Creator by that name;
Our blefs'd Redeemer, God's eternal fon,
Whofe only merits our falvation won,
He did the harmlefs name of fhepherd take,
For our protection, and his mercy's fake,
Which makes thy reft like thofe that reftlefs be,
Like one that is purfued, and cannot flie;
Or like the buffie, buffing, bumming bee,
Or like the fruitlefs naught-refpected flee,
That cuts the fubtile air fo fwift and faft,
Till in the fpidder's web he's fetter'd faft.
So falling faft afleep, and fleeping in a dream,
Down by that dale which flows with milk and cream,
Thy deareft dame did to thee fay,
Francis, Francis, come away;
I wondered when I heard that name begun,
Francis, Francis, that was Adam's fon,

　　　　　　　　　　　　　　　And

And Adam in his time deferv'd no mifreport,
He was the fon of Gilmanfcleugh Robert ;
And Robert was a pretty gentleman,
The heir to James, he was his eldeft fon ;
The firft of Gilmanfcleugh James was then,
Who was the youngeft fon of Thirlfton ;
And John of Thirlfton, I let you know,
Was fon to David Scot of Howpaflaw ;
And David Scot, that worthy man,
Was fon to Sir Walter of the fame ;
For Gilmanfcleugh I've faid enough,
His firft original is from Buckcleugh.
Now of all beafts that ever were or are,
None can for goodnefs with a fheep compare ;
Indeed for bone and burden I muft grant,
He's much inferior to the elephant ;
The dromedarie, camel, horfe, and afs,
For load and carriage doth the fheep furpafs ;
Strong Taurus, Eunoch's fon, the labouring ox,
The ftately ftaig, the bob-tail crafty fox ;
Thefe and all rav'nous beafts of prey muft yield,
Unto the fheep the honour of the field ;
Where fheep abound in Scotland, more or lefs,
There's ftill a part of Jafon's golden fleece.

Dedicated to the worfhipful and truely generous gentleman,

ROBERT SCOT LAIRD OF HORSLIEHILL,
fon to WILLIAM SCOT of Horfliehill, who was
fon to ROBERT SCOT portioner and baillie of
Hawick, who was fon to WILLIAM SCOT, who
was

was fecond fon to the Laird of Midgup ; WAL-
TER SCOT of Midgup was grand-child to ADAM
SCOT of Tuʃhilaw, who was fon to the forefaid
DAVID SCOT of Howpaʃlaw, who was fon to the
firʃt Sir WALTER SCOT of Howpaʃlaw ; their
original was from BUCKCLEUGH.

‘ A SIMPLE ʃheep-ʃkin proves the only tie,
‘ And ʃtay whereon a world of men rely,
‘ Which holds a crew of earth-worms in more awe
‘ Than both the tables of the facred law ;
For as the ram the ewe doth fructify,
And ev'ry year a lamb doth multiply ;
So doth a ʃheep-ʃkin bond make many breed,
And procreate as feed doth fpring from feed,
'Tis one man's freedom and another's lofs,
And, like the Pope, it can both bind and lofe ;
Adám Scot in Delorain I do nominate,
And for thy generation, it cannot be fórgot,
Unto Grafs-yards, thy brother, it is declar'd by me,
Which may ferve all that is of one poʃterity,
And in conclufion this I humbly crave,
That ev'ry one the honeʃty may have,
That when your frail moriality is paʃt,
Ye may be the good ʃhepherds at the laʃt ;
Be not offended at the ʃtile of ʃhepherd fwain,
For Jafon's golden fleece is ʃtill worthy of coin.

❖ ❖

Dedicated to that worthy and valiant Soldier,

CAPTAIN JAMES SCOT, a BRIGADIER in his
Majeʃty's moʃt honourable LIFE-GUARD, fon
to

to WALTER SCOT of Tuſhilaw, who was ſon
to ROBERT SCOT of Tuſhilaw, who was ſon to
Sir WALTER SCOT of Tuſhilaw, who was ſon
to ROBERT SCOT of Tuſhilaw, who was ſon to
ADAM SCOT of Tuſhilaw.

WHOSE former genealogy is already ſpoken ;
   The fable of the golden fleece began,
Becauſe ſheep did yield ſuch ſtore of gold to men;
For he that hath great ſtore of woolly fleeces,
May, when he pleaſes, have ſtore of golden pieces;
Honeſt James Scot of Shiels-wood,
Whoſe like there is not many,
Whoſe love and piety doth feed and help ſo many;
There is no doubt but theſe good deeds of his,
Will help to lift his ſoul to endleſs bleſs ;
Of his genealogy I will ſpeak no more,
Becauſe his brother Grafs-yards is ſet down before;
I hope Jaſon's fleece ſhall never from him flee,
Becauſe he is inclin'd to hoſpitality.

Dedicated to the worthy and much reſpected generous gentleman,

JAMES SCOT OF BRISTO, ſon to Mr JAMES
SCOT, late parſon of Ancrum, who was ſon to
JOHN SCOT of Cachlack-know, who was ſon to
WALTER SCOT of Mount-bernger, who was ſon
to ROBERT SCOT, of Mount-bernger, who was
ſon to SIMON SCOT of Mount-bernger, who was
ſon to SIMON SCOT of Dryhop, who was ſon to
the laird of Howpaſlaw, whoſe original is from
Buckcleugh.
                         MY

MY worthy coufin, I muft to thee commend,
Him who of his talent furely has made ten,
Like as Jofeph did in Egypt long remain,
Whilft his brethren did for food unto him come;
So Gideon privately did live, and made no fcroup,
Whilft that his brethren fwaggred round about;
But now of Jafon's fleece he hath more ftore,
Than ever his brethren had before ;
This Gideon Scot he is a pretty man,
Amongft the reft a worthy fhepherd fwain,
Of Outerfiderig now he is laird,
He was fon to Robert of Har-wood ;
Robert he was a worthy man,
He was fon to Walter of Erckletoun ;
Walter fprung from that fame ftock,
That was call'd John Scot of the New-wark,
And John he was James's fon.
My fleeping mufe is now layen down,
But when fhe wakes out of her dream,
The reft of's pedigree I'll explain ;
Since he and Jafon is fo well acquaint,
His golden fleeces he has to him lent.

Dedicated to that generous and well approved gentleman,

JAMES SCOT, LAIRD OF BOW-HILL.

MIRACULOUS monfters in the Britifh clyme,
Monfters of nature fprung from putrid Shem,
Sampfon that pull'd the gates of Gaza down,
Nor Libian Hercules, whofe furious frown,

P   Would

Would amaze ſtrong giants, tame the lion's rage,
Were not ſo ſtrong as gallants of this age;
Why you ſhall ſee an up-ſtart cock-brain'd Jack,
Will bear five hundred aikers on his back,
And walk as ſtoutly as if it were no load,
And bear it to each place of his abode;
A love-ſick woer would a ſonnet write,
In praiſe of her who was his heart's delight,
Hoping thereby his wiſhed love to win,
And to obtain it, thus he did begin.
 Star of the earth, and empreſs of my ſoul,
Thy love and life, that doth my thoughts controul,
Sole queen of my affections and deſire,
That like to Ætna ſets my heart on fire,
Thy golden locks reſembling Titan's amber,
Moſt fit to grace ſome mighty monarch's chamber:
Thine eyes eclipſing Titan in his riſing,
Thy face ſurpaſſing nature's beſt deviſing,
Thy lips evaporate moſt ſweet perfumes,
Thy voice the muſic of the ſpheres aſſumes;
Perfections wound more than loves ſhaft and bow,
Thy red the roſe doth ſhame, thy white the ſnow,
Thou world's wonder, nature's cleareſt fuel,
Stain not thy virtues with thy being cruel;
Beſides it is an eaſy thing to prove,
It is a ſovereign remedy for love,
As ſuppoſe your thoughts at hourly ſtrife,
Half mad, and almoſt weary of your life;
All for the love of ſome fair female creature,
And that you are intangled with her feature;
' That you are glad, and ſad, and mad, and tame,
' Seeming to burn in froſt, and freeze in flame;
' In one breath, ſinging, laughing, weeping,
' Dream as you walk, and waking in your ſleeping,
Accounting

Accounting hours for years, and months for ages,
Till you enjoy her that your heart engages,
And fhe hath fent you anfwers long before,
That her intent is not to be your whore;
And you, for your part, mean upon your life,
Ne'er while you live to take her to your wife.
The weft-border feed, it is not fit for you,
You may procure better than there doth grow;
Thou art the brother by thy place unto a lovely fwain,
The fon of that renowned fquire, John Scot of Ren-
     nal-burn,
Thy father Robert yet furvives,
Thy goodfire was by the Napiers flain,
Thy grandfire the firft laird of Bow-hill,
Was fon to John Scot of Thirlftone.
A worthy fquire John Scot of Rennal-burn,
He was the fon of that Sir John Scot,
Whom the mufes lov'd, and hovered at his gate.
And Sir John was fon of that learned man,
Mr Arthur Scot who was ftil'd of New-burgh then;
And Mr Arthur was brave Simon's fon,
He who was tutor to the pupils of Thirlftone;
And John of Thirlftone that brave fellow,
Was fon to David Scot of Howpaflaw,
And David was the firft Sir Walter's fon:
So, James with thy genealogy I have done,
And fpoken nothing but the very truth,
Thy original is from Buckcleugh.
Since fates allow the harmlefs beafts fuch ftore,
I hope of Jafon's fleece thou fhalt have more and
     more.

Dedicated to the honourable and truly noble,

SIR WILLIAM ELLIOT OF STOBS,
KNIGHT AND BARONET.

IT's not in expectation of reward,
 That I this book into your hands do render,
But in my humble duty in regard,
That I am bound my dayly thanks to render;
If my verse be defective, and my accent rude,
My stile be harsh, and my learning slender,
I am defended against a multitude,
If that your patronage be but my defender.
This to avoid hell's-hacht ingratitude,
My duteous love, my lines and life shall be
To you devoted ever, to conclude,
May you and your most virtuous lady see
Long happy days, in honour still increasing,
And after death true honour never ceasing.

 Your worship's parents were so well known by me,
That I'm bold to show them to the fourth degree,
These worthy families I must needs commend,
From whom Sir William Elliot of Stobs did descend;
I here set down the number what they are,
And then I'll nominate them in particular.
Thy thirty anceftors I would have men to ken,
Thy eight great-grandsires, and thy eight great-
 grandames,
Thy grandsires and grandames eight, that makes
 twenty-four,
Thy goodsires and goodames four, with father and
 mother;
Thy thirty anceftors I have set down,
And thou thyself makes thirty and and one;

 This

This true account from whence your worſhip ſprung,
Is juſt to the fourth generation of your kin:
Thy firſt great grandſire and grandam, it's of truth,
Was Elliot of Lariſtone and Scot of Buckcleugh;
To thy ſecond great grandſire and grandam now I
 trot,
They were Scot of Hardin, and Scot of Dryhop;
Thy third great grandſire and grandam to their
 name,
Was Douglas of Cavers, and a ſiſter of Cranſton;
Thy fourth great grandſire to his name,
Was Douglas the laird of Whittingham;
I am not certain, yet have heard ſome mean,
He was married to Hepburn a daughter of Waugh-
 ton;
Thy fifth great-grandſire, to whom I flee,
Was Sir John Cranſton and Ramſay of Dalhouſie;
Thy ſixth great-grandſire and grandam, I ſet down,
Was Cranſton of Moriſton and Cockburn of Lan-
 ton;
Thy ſeventh great-grandſire and grandam I reveal,
Was lord Seaton of Seaton and Maxwell of Max-
 well;
Thy eighth great-grandſire and grandam no leſs,
Than Earl Bothwell and Douglas, ſiſter to the Earl
 Angus.
 Now to the firſt grandſire and grandam I come,
Elliot of Stobs and Scot of Hardin;
To the ſecond grandſire and grandam now I run,
Sir William of Cavers, and Douglas of Whitting-
 hame;
Thy third grandſire and grandam I muſt proclaim,
        Was

Was. William Lord Cranſton and Sarah, daughter
     to Sir John ;
Thy fourth grandſire was the, Lord Coldinghame.
   Now thy firſt goodſire I do rehearſe,
Which was Elliot of Stobs and Douglas of Cavers;
Thy other goodſire and goodam of much renown,
Was Mr of Cranſton and daughter to Lord Cold-
     inghame,
Thy father and mother, who ſtill live by fame,
Sir Gilbert of Stobs and ſiſter to Lord Cranſton ;
Although I cannot write, yet I have ſpent my
     breath,
In dilating thy deſcent from good king James the
     Fifth.
Earl Bothwell, thy great-grandſire,
Was a valiant man,
He was king James the Fifth
His own natural ſon.
   And now I humbly crave your worthineſs excuſe
For the boldneſs of my unlearned muſe,
That hath preſum'd ſo high a pitch to flee,
In praiſe of virtue and gentilitie ;
I know this taſk is fit for learned men,
For Homer, Ovid, or for Virgil's pen ;
Boldly to write true honour's worthineſs,
Whilſt better muſes pleas'd to hold their peace ;
And this much to the world my verſe proclaims,
That neither gain nor flattery are my aims ;
But love and duty to your familie
Have cauſed by my muſe theſe lines to publiſh'd be :
And therefore I intreat your generous heart,
To accept my duty and pardon my neglects,---
Bear with my weakneſs, wink at my defects,
Good purpoſes do merit good effects.

Poor earthen veſſels may hold precious wine, _
And I preſume that in this book of mine,
In many places ye ſhall ſomething find,
To pleaſe each noble well affected mind;
And, for excuſe, my muſe doth humbly plead
That ye'll forbear to judge before ye read.

　The Perſians, Egyptians, and the Iſraelites,
And raging Razin, king of Aramites,
Then the Aſſyrians twice, and then again
The Egptians over-run them all amain.
'Then the Chaldeans, and once more they came,
Egyptian Ptolomey, who them o'ercame;
Then Pompey next, king Herod laſt of all,
Veſpaſian was their univerſal fall;
As in Aſſyria monarchy began,
They loſt it to the warlike Perſian;
Of Nimrod's race a race of kings deſcended,
'Till in Aſtiages his ſtock was ended;
For Cyrus into Perſia did tranſlate
The Aſſyrian ſovereign monarchizing ſtate;
'Then after many bloody bruiſing arms,
The Perſian yielded to the Greeks alarms:
But ſmoke-like, Grecian glory laſted not,
Before 'twas ripe it did untimely rot:
The world's commander, Alexander, died,
And his ſucceſſors did the world divide;
From one great monarch in a moment ſprings
Confuſion, hydra-like, from ſelf-made kings;
Till they, all wearied, ſlaughtered and forlorn,
Had all the earth diſmember'd rent and torn;
The Romans took advantage of their fall,
And over-ran, captiv'd, and conquer'd all:
Thus, as none nail another out doth drive,
The Perſians the Aſſyrians did deprive;

　　　　　　　　The

The Grecians then the Perſian pride did tame,
The Romans then the Grecians overcame ;
Whilſt like a vapour all the world was toſt,
And kingdoms were transferr'd from coaſt to coaſt;
And ſtill the Jews, in ſcatter'd multitudes,
Deliver'd were to ſundry ſervitudes,
Chang'd, given, bought, and ſold from land to
    land,
Where they're not underſtood, nor underſtand,
To every monarchy they were made ſlaves,
Egypt, Aram, Chaldea, them outbraves,
Aſſyria, Perſia, Grecia, and laſtly Rome,
Invaded them by heaven's juſt angry doom ;
Four ages did the ſons of Heber paſs,
Before their final diſſolution was ;
Their firſt age, aged patriarchs did guide,
The ſecond reverend judges did decide ;
The third by kings, nought good, bad, worſe and
    worſt,
The fourth by prophets, who them bleſt or curſt,
As their dread God commanded or forbid,
To curſe or bleſs, even ſo the prophets did.
  Good reader, I have writ theſe lines to let thœ
    know withall,
What deſolations did on former ages fall,
And here within ſixſcore of years,
By many families it appears,
Who were men of note, and their ſubſtance did a-
    bound,
Yet to great ſervitude their children came ;
But yet I think men ſhould not fret,
' For a ſuſpenſion never pays no debt ;
For if a man, according to the laws,
He be but captivated for an onerous cauſe,

And

And then from bondage he again return,
This is no act of credit left by him.
In hiftories 'tis often read,
That kings fons have been tradefmen bred ;
Crifpin and Crifpianus the Englifh fing,
Was fon to Brænus the Britifh king,
Of fuch a change men they may admire,
' From a crown to become a cordiner ;
If his fon's fon did live to be a man,
And if that rightly he might play his game,
Durft any paultry pifmee call him down,
' By exclamation to be a futor's fon.
Thefe idle queftionifts, and thefe fchifmatics,
I hold no better than rank heretics ;
But this I think not well when honeft hearts,
Shall have this undervaluing name without deferts;
If every hair upon the heads of men
Were quills, and every quill a pen,
Were earth to paper turn'd, and feas to ink,
And all the world were writers, yet I think
They could not write enough of mifchief's ftrain,
Calumnious boafters, bloody tongued men.
Of Perfians, Pagons, Afians, or Rome,
' I need not write, there's divifion enough at home.
  For the Elliots brave and worthy men,
Have been as much opprefs'd as any name I ken,
For in my own time I have feen fo much odds,
No Elliot enjoyed any heritage, but Dunlibire, Fa-
  nafh, and Stobs ;
Stobs being *fine qua non*, and obedient to the truth,
A beloved fifter-fon to the family of Buckcleugh :
Yet in the border-fide the Elliots did remain,
Since King Robert the firft, they with him from
  Angus came.

          Q   The

The town of Elliot was their antiquitie,
Which ftands in Angus in the foot of Glenfhie;
With brave king Robert the Bruce they hither came,
Which is three hundred and eighty-years agone;
In weft Tiviotdale thefe gentlemen did dwell,
They were twelve great families, I heard my good-
    fire tell;
Their chief was then a baron of renown,
Defigned Reidheugh, which is now call'd Lariftone;
Stobs and Dunlibyre is of the ancient kind,
Cobfhaw, Brugh, Prickinhaugh, and Gorinberrie's
    gone,
Yet there's more Elliots by other ftiles that fupply
    their room;
Erckletoun it was long out of Elliots name,
But now it is return'd to the felf fame again;
Elliot of Bewlies, fome fay, he's not a gentleman;
But I proteft they do him wrong to his ninth ge-
    neration;
What, if a man have fons three,
Procreate and born from one belly,
Can one of them be a gentleman,
And another be a peafant's fon?
' He neither defcends from kill nor mill,
He's fprung from the laird of Horfliehill,
Thereof his grandfire was a younger brother-fon,
Though he was fervant to the laird of Hardin;
Hardin the forefaid William did fo much efteem,
That he in marriage his natural daughter did gain,
And betwixt them two was procreat, I muft reveal,
That Robert Elliot that lived in Borthwickfheill;
And Robert Elliot married a gentle dame,
Hately from the family of Mellarftain,
                          Betwixt

Betwixt them two was procreat fure,
Good Thomas Elliot in Borthwickfheils,
That much reliev'd the poor;
And Thomas Elliot married then,
The daughter of the laird chamberlain Newton,
And procreat betwixt them be
William Elliot of Bewlie;
William Elliot of Bewlie, ye underftand the man,
He's married with the fifter of Scot of Sinton,
' Who him calumniates with a mif-report,
' I'll fay he is a liar in his throat;
For Romulus that builded Rome,
Was nurs'd upon a bear yet was a prince's fon;
The father of the faithful, Abram, Abel and Lot,
Were fhepherds in their time, yet types and pa-
        triarchs;
The Scythian fhepherd, a conqueror compleat,
Tammerlane the great, yet he attended fheep;
He is but *mala fama* whatever be his coin,
That fays that Bewlie is not a gentleman:
Walter of Erckletoun thefe mif-reports may clear,
For he was called nothing but fhepherd forty year;
And yet he is the juft and very man,
Whofe goodfir and grandfir was lairds of Erckleton;
Even though Horfliehill were to fell at this time,
And William Elliot were he that fhould it gain,
It were but a fufpenfion he had underline,
Being truely defcended from that felf fame kind;
And though that his grandfir was a fervant man,
For the want of means to the laird of Hardin;
And he by his fervice and good hufbandry,
Had purchafed means might fet Horfliehill free;
But being not to fell, he purchas'd other lands,
' Doth that make out that he's not a gentleman?

The

The Elliots of the Yare they are of that fame kind,
And the Elliots of Selkirk they are of the fame.
If James Elliot late of Bridgeheugh, be a gentle-
man,
Then William Elliot of Bewlie muft needs be one;
For their grandfirs were two brother-fons,
Though in occupation there was defference,
The one a magiftrate in Selkirk town,
The other kept the fheep upon the Doun;
The one did live by polling of the poor,
Being magiftrate was counted great honour:
The other was a fhepherd fwain, and reliev'd the
poor that came,
With bed and board, though but a fervant man.
Sixty-years ago I have both heard and feen,
And knew that Robert was the laird of Hardin's
man;
Yet he was the poors relief,
For he fed and clad them both with flefh and fleece;
But for the magiftrate few poor he did relieve,
He was ftill ready to take but never to give:
' Sir Baillie, if't pleafe your worfhip,
Was the word of every one;
The other was Will or Hab,
Yet both from brethren came;
Their forefaid marriages they are fet down by me,
To be a truth I will affirm, and that they are no lie;
I have both eat and drunk, and merry with them
been,
All of them except the firft William,
Which my father knew and that very well,
To be of the family of thefe of Horfliehill;
And fince Horfliehill was thy fore-fathers ftile,
Bewlie it hath been the fame for a pretty while:

And

And I ftill do wifh that ftile do remain,
With thee and with thine, till the period of time:
Yet pardon my lines, though they be out of frame,
For I could never any write but the letters of my
　　name;
And although that they be not pleafant to the view,
Yet they are both honeft, modeft, chafte, and true;
And though Jafon fetch'd his golden fleece from
　　Greece,
Thy fleece in Scotland it is many poors relief.

Dedicated to the very honourable, and much refpected generous gentleman,

THE LAIRD OF LARISTON.

COULD my unpractis'd pen advance thy name,
　Thou fhould be mounted on the wings of
　　fame,
Thy anceftors they were of good renown,
They being all the lairds of Larifton;
Into thy hands I do commit the fum
Of Walter Elliot of Erlketon,
By Maxwell's rage out of their hands it got,
And was poffefs'd by Cunninghame and Scot;
Now Providence has brought it back again,
To the lineal heir of Elliot's kind;
For Walter Elliot he was Adam's fon,
And Adam's goodfire was laird of Erkleton;
Tho' they were fufpended for an age or twain,
The lands return'd to Elliot of Muckildine;
He is the laird of Erkleton's brother,
And Janet Scot fhe is Muckildine's mother,

　　　　　　　　　　　A worthy

A worthy wife fhe of long time hath been,
And hath fill'd many a poor and hungry wame ;
She is my friend, therefore I do her ken,
She's daughter to John Scot, call'd of Rennalburn,
An honeft gentleman, he was known well enough,
In Efdailmuir he was baillie to Buckcleugh,
' Who was fon to John Scot, an able lad,
' Who then was called Jocky ill to had ;
His father alfo he was called John,
He was natural fon to Scot of Thirlfton,
He was natural brother in the while
To Thirlfton, Newburgh, and Bowhill,
Gilmanfcleugh, Hundelfhope, and Kirkhope,
Were all brethren to the faid John Scot ;
Thefe feven brethren were ftout valiant men,
They would not been afraid for other ten ;
No more of Muckildine, fince Adam is deceaft,
Who left them ftore like Jafon's golden fleece.

Dedicated to the very worthy and valourous gentleman,

WILLIAM ELLIOT OF DUNLIBIRE, Esq;

I Humbly now, according to my dream,
   Prefent to you the young laird of Erkleton,
From's goodfire and grandfire that land was reft
      and riven,
Before they purchas'd coin to buy it back again ;
And now 'tis their own, I wifh they may't enjoy,
From envy's canker, better than Helen did Troy ;
                                    That

That Trojan and that Greek that fought in Samos
    fand,
Achilles gain'd the day, and did Hector command;
Troy's fruitful queen did many children bear,
So brave, heroic, and fo ftout a crew,
Who all in noble actions did accrue;
When age had made their parents bald and bare,
They made their dauntlefs courage to appear,
Amidft the throngs of danger and debate,
But blood on blood their fury could not fate:
In former times the South may underftand,
Many gallants lofed all their land,
Through blood, and want of government,
Which to this time fucceffors may repent;
They were not like thefe Arcadians in Greece,
That rejoic'd in Jafon's golden fleece.

✳✤✤✤✤✤✤✤✤✤✤✤✤✤✤✤✤✤✤✤✤✤✤✤✳

Dedicated to that worthy and generous gentleman,

ROBERT ELLIOT, LAIRD OF MIDLIEMILL.

SIR, in my fleep I was much troubled,
   And dream'd of Henry Elliot of Harewood,
'Mongft many more that I thought I faw,
And knowing he was your father-in-law,
Therefore my weak judgement thought it fit,
Thefe lines to you that I fhould dedicate;
Knowing him to be a worthy man,
And much honour'd by your generation;
Though all in one you now joined be,
Yet ye're a pear grew higher on the tree;

                         For

For I believe there is fo much odds,
Few Elliots compared with the houfe of Stobs;
For heaven's high hand where he doth pleafe to
    blefs;
Make trees, or men fruitful, or fruitlefs;
In fundry ufes trees do ferve mens turn,
To build, adorn; to feed, or elfe to burn;
Thus is mens ftate in all degrees like theirs,
Some are got to the top of honour's ftairs,
Securely fleeping on opinion's pillow;
Yet is as fruitlefs as the fruitlefs willow,
And fill up room, like worthlefs trees in woods,
Whofe goodnefs confifts all in ill-got goods;
He like a cedar makes a goodly fhow,
But no good fruit will from his greatnefs grow,
Until he die and from his goods depart,
And then gives all away in fpight of his heart;
' Then fhall his friends with mourning clothes be
    clad,
' The infide merry, and the outfide fad;
He thinks his life angelical, becaufe
Among the angels he his time doth pafs;
And with his nobles he ordaineth laws,
That bafe extortion fhall not be a crime;
He marks how kingdoms, provinces, and towns.
Are over-ruled by his curfed crowns,
But if he note his angels what to be,
Not heavenly, nor thefe from heaven that fell,
But they are in a third and worfe degree,
Damn'd fenflefs monfters, even that are of hell,
They cannot hear, feel, tafte, or fmell,
A thoufand times being told yet cannot tell;
They're lock'd and barr'd, and bolted up in thrall,
Which fhows their nature not angelical;
                   Thy

Thy induftrious loyalty doth daily tell,
Thou aims at honour and thou levels well,
And with your trufty fervice fhot complete,
That in the end you fure will hit the whyte ;
Thus thy induftries doth let the world ken,
That Jafon's golden fleece with thee fhall ftill re-
　　main.

Dedicated to that worthy and well approved gentleman,

JOHN ELLIOT, Brother to Sir WILLIAM EL-LIOT of Stobs.

GOOD Sir, if fortune frown or fmile thou art
　　content,
Thou bears a heart that is ftill ready bent ;
God is thy Captain, thy defence and hold,
Through faith in him thou art ftill armed bold ;
To thank John Elliot I humbly thee defire,
He dwells in Unthank, he's brother to Dunlibire :
When kind kiffing Phœbus was gone to her reft,
In a winter's night in a moft furious blaft,
I driving beafts, becaufe I wanted fodder,
I did affault his houfe into tempeftuous weather ;
For god Æolus blew, and Boreas did affift,
And Neptune's watery planets he broke in betwixt,
The fnow being deep, the fnow tempeftuous ill,
I was five days in driving twenty mile ;
In great diftrefs into his houfe I came,
He with his wife made me kindly welcome,
With bed and board, good brandy and good ale,
Which might have ferv'd the beft in Tiviotdale.

　　　　　　R　　　　　　　I wifh

I wiſh John Elliot may never want ſuch fleeces,
Which yearly may bring in ten thouſand golden
    pieces.

Dedicated to that much renowned generous gentleman,

WILLIAM ELLIOT, Uncle to Sir WILLIAM EL-
LIOT of Stobs.

MOST worthy Sir, I hope I do no wrong,
    In dedicating to you one of my ſhepherd
    ſwains;
Take not a ſhepherd ſwain to be a vulgar name,
For kings and emperors have gloried in the ſame;
Therefore no ſhepherd ſwain my muſe ſhall e'er
    deride,
And far leſs William Elliot, the good laird of
    Swoonſide,
Since thou art worthy and a lovely one,
Not like envy, all conſum'd to ſkin and bone.
Sir, I do declare what labour thou haſt ſpent,
Was neither to honour nor virtue's detriment;
And thrice worthy Sir, thy virtues do proclaim,
How honour's noble mark it is ſtill thy aim;
And when thou the head-ſtrong Taurus ſoon for-
    ſakes,
And to his ſummering progreſs thou haſte makes,
Then ſhall the earth's celeſtial light afford,
And in ſad darkneſs clad the ample globe;
Since I was born, when wit was out of town,
That's the reaſon that I have ſo little of my own;
                      Pardon

Pardon me, I cannot write, and very little read,
Or elfe in thy worthy praife I farther would pro-
　　ceed;
As for Swoonfide, I wifh his golden fleece
May fhine as bright as Jafon's did in Greece.

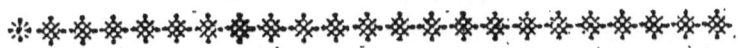

Dedicated to that virtuous and well approven gentleman,

Mr GAVIN ELLIOT, Uncle to Sir WILLIAM
　　　ELLIOT of Stobs.

MOST worthy Sir, according to my dream,
　　　I fpeak of fhepherds, and of fhepherd fwains;
Into your gentle hands, Sir, I do commit,
John Elliot, the laird of Thorilfhope;
And Sir, I do hope that ye'll not difallow,
That I have been fo bold as dedicate him to you;
For a man muft more than human wit poffefs,
To efcape the baits and fnares of wickednefs:
The artift of the fcripture can difpute the fame,
That one would deem him a religious man;
Since that God gave life to herbs, and plants, and
　　　trees,
A beaft hath fenfe, and life, moves, feels, and fees,
For if they wanted life, how could they then grow?
And, in fome fort, both good and evil know;
But man he is before all creatures in degrees,
God life, fenfe, and reafon unto him gives;
And leaft that thefe bleffings fhould be tranfitory,
He gave him life and fenfe, reafon, grace, and glory;
So I hope Thorilfhope fhall keep his golden fleece,
As glorious as Jafon did his in Greece.

Dedicated to that worthy and complete gentleman,

ROBERT ELLIOT, Appearant of DUNLIBIRE.

MOST worthy Sir, I do upon the wings of fame,
    Dedicate to you one of your worthy name,
John Elliot, he who's call'd a valiant lad,
He's brother to Henry Elliot of Harewood ;
It was into my dream he did appear to me,
For I into the ale-house did him never fee ;
In Jafon's golden fleece it's faid he doth abound,
And now he is of late a perfon much renown'd,
Therefore I do him confecrate to thee,
And with happinefs to you and your pofterity,
Wifhing to him, when he his fheep doth fhear,
They may improve their fleece four times a year,
For that man that hath ftore of wool, and woolly
      fleeces,
May, when he pleafes, have ftore of gold and gold-
     en pieces.

✢✢✢✢✢✢✢✢✢✢✢✢✢✢✢✢✢✢✢✢✢✢✢✢✢

Dedicated to that valorous and complete young gentleman,

ROBERT ELLIOT, Appearant of LARISTON.

SIR, thefe lines unto your hand I fend,
    Wifhing your worfhip will but them commend,
And begs that you'll not be agaft,
For nominating fome firft that fhould be laft ;
Therefore, good Sir, I hope you will pardon give,
And oblige your humble fervant while he lives ;
                   This

This I lay open to your worſhip's view,
And Simon Elliot of Tarras I dedicate to you ;
For ſummer-fruit it is pleaſant to eat,
But winter it will a long time keep ;
Although the hills of Tarras they be black,
Yet in his golden fleece there is no lack ;
Black moiſty fleeces, when they are well ſcour'd,
Unto the owners yield good, clear, and current gold.
Pure Spaniſh gold it's very fine,
But of wool our merchants make more gain ;
Through Chriſtendom your woolly fleeces,
Are ſtill compar'd to golden pieces ;
So he that is a ſhepherd ſwain,
Can be no leſs than a gentleman :
Monarchs and kings, royal majeſtie,
Were ſhepherd ſwains in Arcadie.

Dedicated to the young and very hopeful gentleman,

GILBERT ELLIOT, Son to Sir WILLIAM EL-
LIOT of STOBS, Knight Baronet.

IF Homer's verſe in Greek did merit praiſe,
  If Naſo in the Latin tongue wan bayes,
If Maro 'mongſt the Romans did excel,
If Taſſo in the Tuſcan tongue ſpoke well :
Sweet Sir, pardon him that's ſo much unperfeĉt,
In Scots can ſcarcely read, and never could yet
    write ;
If my poor ſhallow brain could but advance your
    name,
Ye ſhould be mounted high upon the wings of fame;
                                              And

And if that my poor thoughts had ftrength to en-
    terprize;
I would advance your name as far as Titan's rife,
And that fhepherd fwain that I do fimulize,
Is Robert Elliot that dwells in the Dewflies :
Be not offended at the name of fhepherd fwain,
For formerly that name was noblemen ;
And as Jafon fetcht his golden fleece from Greece,
I wifh that Robert Elliot his fleeces may increafe.

*Dedicated to the very honourable, and right worfhipful gene-
rous gentleman,*

JOHN HOPPRINGLE, LAIRD OF TORSONCE.

IF the value of offerings are always to be equal
to the grandeur of the perfons to whom they
are prefented, I fhould not dare to make this bold
addrefs; but the greatnefs of my devotion, that
hath no other way to manifeft itfelf at prefent,
will, I hope, make amends for the meannefs of this,
and perfuade your worfhip to condefcend to the acceptance of this poor expreffion of my refpects ; if
thefe treatifes may be fo happy as to give unto
your worfhip fome fatisfaction and recreation in
the perufal of them, I fhall attain unto the advantage which is chiefly aimed at by this dedication,
    Your worfhip's moft obedient, moft humble,
      and faithful fervant,
            WALTER SCOT.

                    MOST

MOST worthy Sir, ye know this well by me,
   That the love of brandy made myfelf mer-
   rie,
For when the high-born baftard of the thundring
   Jove,
When men's inventions are of wit moft hollow,
He with his fprightful juice their fp'rits doth move,
To the harmonious mufic of Apollo,
' And, in a word, I would have all men know it,
' He muft drink brandy that means to be a poet:
I underftand, or know no foreign tongue,
But their tranflations I do much admire,
Much art, much pains, much ftudy it doth require,
And at the leaft regard fhould be their hire ;
When Adam was in Paradife firft placed,
And with the rule of mortal things was graced,
Then rofes, pinks, and fragrant gilly-flowers,
Adorn'd and deck'd forth Eden's bleffed bowers ;
Love is a dying life, and living death ;
A vapour, fhaddow, a bubble, and a breath,
An idle bable, and a paultry toy,
Whofe greateft patron is a blinded boy ;
But pardon love, my judgment is unjuft,
For what I fpeak of love I mean of luft ;
' Befs fhe diflikes the furplice and the cap,
' And calls them idle veftments of the Pope ;
' And miftrefs Maud would go to church right fain,
' But that the corner cap makes her refrain ;
' And Madam Idle is offended deep,
' The preacher fpeaks fo loud fhe cannot fleep ;
Lo thus the devil fowes contentions feed,
Whence fects, and fchifms, and herefies do breed ;
Since Providence has given you wit in ftore,
Live as your worthy fathers did live you before.

By

By night I in a vifion did dream,
That four and twenty fhepherds I had feen,
Whereof John Andifon was one ;
A fhepherd fwain that dwells at Thirlftone ;
A civil perfon, and one that is true,
And therefore I dedicate him to you ;
I hope the name of fhepherd ye'll not defpife it,
Since kings and princes hath it enterprifed,
Befides, the learned poets of all times,
Have chanted out their praife in pleafant rhymes,
The harmlefs lives of rural fhepherd fwains,
And beauteous fhepherdeffes on the plains ;
They have recorded moft delightfully,
Their love, their fortune, and felicity ;
And fure if in this low terreftrial round,
Plain honeft happinefs is to be found,
It with the fhepherd is remaining ftill,
Becaufe they have leaft power to do ill ;
And whilft they on the feeding flocks attend,
They have the leaft occafion to offend ;
I wifh God blefs the fhepherds and their fleeces,
And then I hope they'll ne'er want golden pieces.

****

*Dedicated to the very honourable, and right worfhipful gene-
rous gentleman,*

JOHN RIDDEL OF HAINING,

Sheriff-principal of the fheriffdom of Selkirk, and
Provoft of that Burgh-royal.

I Humbly wifh peace, truth, and conftancy,
Remain with you and your worthy family ;

That

That failor gains renown that well does know,
To gain his point either at ebb or flow,
When Boreas' duft doth drive thee from the land,
Then Æolus' blafts puts thee in Neptune's hand;
To wonder and admire is all one thing,
As fynonymies the word betake;
But if a double meaning from them come,
For double fenfe your judgement then muft look;
As once a man all foul'd with dirt and myre,
Fell down and wondered not, but did admire;
To you whofe ears, and eyes have heard and feen,
This little pamphlet, and can judge between
That which is good, tolerable, or ill,
May be with artlefs nature wanting fkill:
Have I writ ought that may your hearts content,
My mufe hath then accomplifht her intent,
Your favour can preferve me, but your frown
My poor inventions in oblivion drown;
With tolerable friendfhip let me crave,
You will not feek to fpill what you may fave.
The Afp that quakes with fun,
He doth me much deride,
' The Webfter and the Smith,
' They fhake their brainlefs head,
And fay, my education, or my ftate
Doth make my verfe efteem'd at lower rate;
To fuch as thofe, this anfwer I do fend,
And bid them mend before they difcommend;
Their envy unto me will favours prove,
The hatred of fools breeds wife mens love;
My mufe is jocund, that her labours merits
To be malign'd and fcorn'd by envyous carriage.
This humbly I beg pardon of the beft,
Which being granted, Sir, a reverence for the reft.
　　　　S　　　　　　　　Why

Why fhould they vex in their malicious brain,
For I have done no wrong to you nor them;
A greedy wretch did on the fcripture look,
Found it recorded in the facred book,
How fuch a man with God fhould fure prevail,
Who clad the naked, and vifited them in jail,
And there he found how he had long miftaked,
And oftentimes had made the cloathed naked;
In ftead of vifiting the oppreft in moans,
He had confum'd them to the very bones;
Yet one day he at leifure would repent,
But fudden death repentance did prevent;
Then he was dead and laid into his tomb,
In hopes repentance from purgatory come;
There lay the Stuart of the valiant ten,
Who, whilft on life his beloved life remain'd;
Apollo's daughter, and the heirs of Jove,
The memorable bounty did approve;
His life was life to Statius, and his death
Bereav'd the mufes of celeftial breath;
Had Phœbus fir'd him from the lofty fkies,
That Phenix-like another might arife,
From out of his odoriferous facred embers,
His loved life the country ftill remembers;
Amongft a million there is hardly any,
That like yourfelf, fo well can govern many.
Now I think well I will reveal,
My dream I muft proclaim,
And dedicate unto your hands, my honeft fhep-
  herd's fwain,
That merrily upon the plain doth fing with jok-
  ing lees,
His fhepherdefs fhe does not mifs to crown his head
  with bayes;
         Love,

Love, bounty, valour, charity with shepherds did
 remain,
It's Kings and Emperors liberty to be a shepherd
 swain,
In meadows green where flowers do spring,
There they do feed their flocks,
Sometimes on mountains and on hills,
Sometimes amongst the rocks;
Their worthy generosity to love is a strong fort,
With triumph doth that trumpet sound,
At the shepherd swain's port,
The best of men are shepherd swains,
As I before design'd,
The eastern coasts did brag and boast,
Of their brave shepherd swain;
George Curror's then a shepherd swain,
That gains both corn and store,
And doth afford both bed and board,
And much relieves the poor;
In Hartwoodmyres his barns and byers,
And shepherds do remain,
His flocks proceed, and swiftly feed
Upon the morning dew;
And when bright Phœbus takes her coach,
They are in Haining's view,
Of that shepherd's truth I cannot dite enough,
But now I'm run ashore;
For shepherd swains, their ewes and lambs,
I have spoken much before;
Though Jason fetcht his fleece from Greece,
And was call'd the golden swain,
George Curror that dwells in Hartwoodmyres,
For wool more gilt doth gain.

       Dedicated

Dedicated to the learned and well approved generous gentleman,

ANDREW PLUMMER, LAIRD OF MIDDLESTEAD.

Most worthy Sir, Sedition and Commonwealth was intimated by two lobsters, fighting one with another ; the land lobster is a great enemy to the serpents and snakes ; therefore the E-gyptian priests did put it to signify a temperate man, who suppresseth his lusts and wicked affections, that are the most dangerous serpents unto his soul.

THIS pamphlet I send to your view,
   Is to let your worship ken,
It's known to be the first issue
Of my dull idle brain ;
It's known as yet, I could ne'er write,
My reading is but small,
For refuge, I flee to your hands,
In hopes you'll warrand all ;
Shepherds I thought were three times eight,
Appear'd into my dream,
Wherefore one to you I dedicate,
A civil honest man ;
He in Analshope doth dwell,
His name's Michael Andison ;
That shepherd swain will no man wrong,
In religion he is strong ;
The foulest fiends assume the fairest forms,
The fairest fields do feed the foulest toad,
The sea at calmest most subject is to storms,
In choicest fruit the canker makes abode ;
So in the shop of all believing trust,
Lyes toads invenom'd, treason couched fast,

Till

Till like a ſtorm his toothleſs thoughts outburſt,
Who, canker like, had lyen in truſt's repoſe ;
For as the fire within the flint's confin'd,
In deepeſt ocean ſtill unquench'd remains ;
Even ſo the falſe, though trueſt ſeeming mind,
Deſpight of truth the treaſon ſtill retains,
Yet maugure treaſon, truth deſerveth truſt,
And truſt ſurvives when treaſon dies accurſt :
Since Michael Andiſon hath great ſtore of woolen
    fleece,
I wiſh they more abound than Jaſon's did in Greece.

Dedicated to that valiant and generous gentleman,

JAMES GLADSTAINS of that Ilk, LAIRD of
    COCKLAW.

MOST worthy Sir, I ſend into your view,
   This little pamphlet, moſt of it is true ;
According to my dream, I yet commend,
I know no fooliſh man can you offend ;
Of four and twenty ſhepherds I did dream,
Whereof James Grieve in Commonſide was one,
An honeſt man you know it ſure,
And one that doth relieve the poor ;
Your generous noble ſp'rit, as I do underſtand,
Emboldens me to dedicate him to your hand ;
He that may hunt on every incloſed ground,
A park of's own he needeth not to found ;
The ſtately ſtag when he his horns hath ſhed,
In ſullen ſadneſs he deplores his loſs ;
But when a wife cornuts her huſband's head,
His gains in horns he holds an extreme croſs ;
                           ' The

' The ftag of lofing, doth his lofs complain,
' The man by gaining doth lament his gain :
Thus whether horns be either loft or found,
They both the lofer and the winner wound.
Hunting is pleafant, but yet wearifome
To him that can no venifon obtain ;
Thou worthy fwain choofe in Diana's ftream,
Amongft the fifters nine, and pick out one of them,
Wit, courage, valour, ftature, and ftate,
Remain with thee, don't fear a horned pate :
Now, good James Grieve, I wifh thy flocks increafe,
That thou may chant and fing, and ftill keep Ja-
     fon's fleece.

*Dedicated to the very worthy and much refpected generous
gentleman,*

ROBERT LANGLANDS OF THAT ILK.

WHen fond imaginary dreams do ring,
   In formlefs forms in mens molefted brain,
On fuch a time, I fleeping in my bed,
An unaccuftom'd dream came in my head ;
I thought four and twenty to me came,
All gentlemen and fhepherd fwains,
Whereof James Grieve, Lenup, he was one,
Which I have dedicated unto your worfhip's hand ;
You know him well to be an honeft man,
And is a juft and harmlefs fhepherd fwain ;
His fleece doth clothe the naked, that there's none
    deny,
His food relieves the needy as they pafs him by,
              The

The orphan, widow, and the indigent,
For bed and board from him have fupplement.
Thefe fhepherd fwains, as I do underftand,
Relieve more poor than all the lairds of the land ;
Their butter, cheefe, their milk, their whey,
Their flefh and wool they part continually,
That I dare fay, were there not fuch men,
Five thoufand in the year would ftarve and pine :
God blefs their fubftance that help the poor folks
 meffes,
And fend them ftore of wool to bring them golden
 pieces.

****

Dedicated to the worthy and much refpected gentleman,

FRANCIS GLADSTAINS OF WHITLAW.

MOST worthy Sir, do not difdain,
 That I my dream fo oft explain ;
Unto your hands I do it commit,
The iffue of a barren wit ;
A great deal more from me might appear,
Within this feventy and two year,
But what is paft I cannot now recall,
I hope ye'll think this makes amends for all :
I never was at fchool, I cannot write,
Pardon my lines though they be unperfyte ;
The beft of gallants indeed may controul,
A wife man will ever countenance a fool,
Although in wrong he will not bear him up,
Yet he will laugh at his foolifh fate ;
The four and twenty of my dream,
William Grieve of Commonfide was one,

    Which

Which I have dedicate to you,
He is an honeſt man and true;
A worthy ſhepherd ſwain, who lives upon his ſtore.
And relieves the poor and needy, as I have ſaid before.
I wiſh his golden fleece with him may ſtill remain,
While I fetch Jaſon's fleece from Greece into
      Scotland.

****

Dedicated to the generous, and much reſpeĉted gentleman,

WALTER SCOT OF BURNFOOT.

MOST worthy Sir, according to my dream,
    Into this pamphlet remains to be ſeen,
I hope your goodneſs will allow,
That I dedicate Walter Grieve to you;
He is a true and honeſt man,
He's both your neighbour and ſhepherd ſwain;
One dedication might have ſerv'd for all,
What I have ſaid before, to mention it again,
It is a needleſs labour, and puts the writer to more
      pain;
I wiſh you meikle joy of all your golden pieces,
And like to Walter Grieve, with increaſe of his
      fleeces.

Dedicated

Dedicated to his worthy, and well respected good friend,

FRANCIS SCOT, BROTHER GERMAN TO THE LAIRD OF BURNFOOT IN AIL.

SIR, this pamphlet to your hands I send,
In hopes that ye will it commend;
For pens ye know I can use none,
I can hardly read the catechism;
Yet four and twenty shepherds,
I saw into my dream,
Whereof good Thomas Anderson,
In Howfoord he was one;
Seeing ye are a gentleman, and my friend,
I have dedicate him into your hand:
When Jupiter the son of Saturn
Had put his father to the flight,
The Empire of the world he did divide then,
Betwixt himself and his brother Neptune;
Neptune set Pluto for to dwell in Hell,
Amongst the priests where still they do rebel;
The sacred records they do demonstrate,
The idols which the Israelites did prostrate,
So do we find into the present time,
That there are priests of every kind,
Kings, prophets, priests, all were shepherd swains,
And did attend all kind of sheep,
Both weathers, ewes, and lambs:
For Thomas Anderson I wish his flocks may still a-
bound,
If Jason lost his golden fleece, I'm sure he has it found.

T   *Dedicated*

Dedicated to the worſhipful and very much reſpected and generous gentleman,

HENRY FORRESTER OF STONEGIRTHSIDE,

in the kingdom of England, juſtice of peace and coram in the ſaid kingdom, in the reign of King Charles the ſecond.

COME, Pamphlet, take thy wings, flee from
      my hand,
Arrive in England, in the county of Cumberland,
There ſtands a houſe, and that a worthy one,
By Kerſupfoot in the eye of the ſun;
A ſtately building, all of plain hew'n ſtone,
All built within this year or twain,
All Cumberland, except caſtle and abbay,
Such another houſe in proſpect you'll not ſee;
Unto that Engliſh ſquire I dedicate
Honeſt John Robertſon, he was born in the Flat;
His father was an Engliſh man,
Francis Robſon kept good order,
There was no Engliſh compar'd with him,
Seven mile within the border;
Juſtice Forreſter an Engliſh ſquire,
And John Robſon a Scot,
Yet it is ſcarce a mile betwixt,
Where they were born and got;
It's true John Robſon is
A comrade good enough,
And for houſe keeping he excels,
He dwells in Cauterſcleugh,
Wheat bread and ſalt beef,
Good mutton and old cheeſe,

A

As I was riding by,
He did my hungar eafe,
He feafted me in May, as I had been an earl,
With capon and good lamb, brandy and good ale;
And for his father Francis,
I knew him well enough
To be a gentleman, ftore-mafter
To Walter Earl of Buckcleugh:
I wifh that Jafon's fleece
With him may ftill appear,
And that his flocks would change
Their coats twelve times a year.

****

Dedicated to that worthy and generous gentleman,

JOHN SCOT, APPEARAND OF HEADSHAW.

I Thought four and twenty fhepherd fwains,
  In my dream I did fee,
Whereof I have dedicated one of them to thee;
John Grieve of Garwald a right honeft one,
Which relieves the poor, and proves a Chriftian
      man;
And with his fmall fubftance he is well content,
Though in late times he prov'd a puritant.
I wifh his fleeces be no worfe,
Than Jafon's fleeces were in Greece.

T 2   *Dedicated*

Dedicated to the right Reverend, and truely pious, and vertuous
generous gentleman.

MR RICHARD SCOT, PARSON OF ASKIRK.

THESE lines, good Sir, I present to your hand,
Is a genealogy of the old family of Sinton,
Which yourself doth represent I know,
Except your nephew the laird of Bonraw;
It is four hundred winters past in order,
Since that Buckcleugh was warden in the border;
A son he had at that same tide,
Which was so lame could neither run nor ride,
The laird wist not what to do with him,
For border service he was fit for none;
At his place call'd Scotstoun,
He did there remain,
Four ages, or he went to Mordistoun;
And since he went, I can make appear,
It is more nor three hundred years:
John his lam'd son,
If my author speak true,
He sent him to St Mungo's in Glasgow,
Where he remain'd a scholar's time,
Then married a wife according to his mind,
And betwixt them two was procreat,
Both sons and daughters of the name of Scot,
What time his posterity did there remain,
My author says to the third generation;
Yet from that stock there sprung a man,
That was the Archbishop's chamberlain,
A quick mettel'd little man,
For which they call'd him Wat the Ratten:

This

This worthy Ratten did begin,
When Robert call'd Fern-year was Scotland's king;
The bishop lov'd Wat well enough,
And recommended him to Buckcleugh,
His chamberlain he did continue still,
And at the Burnfoot in Aill
He built both kill and mill,
Then down the water he fought with speed,
And married Headshaw's daughter,
Her name was Shortreid;
And betwixt them two was procreat,
Headshaw, Aſkirk, Sinton, and Glack;
George was the firſt did Sinton's ſweet knows flock,
He married Turnbull's daughter,
The knight of Falſhope;
Walter his ſon was call'd a pretty man,
He married with Scot the laird of Haſſindean;
John, Walter's ſon, I have heard relation,
Married the laird of Riddel's daughter,
And died without ſucceſſion;
Walter ſucceeded his brother John,
And married a daughter of the laird of Johnſton;
Then George he was Walter's ſon,
He married Scot daughter to the laird of Roberton;
This George he was the very man
That was father to Sinton, Whitſlade, and Hardin,
For Walter he was George's Son,
The elder brother of William of Hardin;
This Walter Scot, ye's underſtand,
He married Cockburn daughter of Henderland,
And betwixt them they got one only ſon,
The lady died when ſhe was but young;
Their ſon Walter did to Riddel ride,
And took the laird's daughter to his bride;

His father Walter was not an old man,
He married another daughter of Riddel's then,
And left Sinton unto his fon ;
And then in Whitflade he fat down,
Betwixt him and Margaret Riddel was procreate
Twelve bairns that were all married ;
Robert of Whitflade was their firft fon,
And William of Huntly was his brother-german,
James of Satchels he was nieft,
And Thomas of Whithaugh-brae made up the
    meffe.
The eight daughters I'll let you ken,
The eldeft was the lady Black-Ormfton,
So was the lady Langlands, and the lady Tofturn-
    bull ;
The lady Ailmour fhe was next,
And the goodwife of the Fanafh,
And the lady Chapel-Middelmifs ;
The youngeft I have almoft forgot,
She was firft married to Philip of Kirkup,
He was a brother to Robert of Thirleftone :
Then fhe was married to Walter Scot of Wall,
But to neither of them fhe bore chiidren ;
Then Alexander Chifholm of Park-hill did her gain,
And to him fhe bare twelve or thirteen bairns.
  Now my wearied mufe, thou haft been long a-
    ftray,
Thefe are the firft Whitflade's pofterity ;
Now to George Howcoat I muft return,
He was young Walter of Sinton's fon,
A brave houfe-keeper, a worthy man,
He married Adimfton, daughter to the laird of Ed-
    nam ;
                  Then

Then Walter Scot was George Howcoat's fon,
He married Douglas, a daughter of Whitting-
　　hame,
And George his fon, a hopeful lad,
He married Gladftains, daughter to the laird of
　　Dode,
There was procreat betwixt thefe two,
Good Mr George Scot, the laird of Bonraw;
George of Bonraw married was
To Douglas a brother daughter of Cavers,
And there is procreate betwixt them twa,
This prefent young laird of Boonraw:
Moft reverend Sir, I hope you'll pardon me,
For waiding fo deep in your genealogie:
If any man think he can amend it,
Poor Wattie Scot fhall never be offended.

∽∽∽∽∽∽∽∽∽∽

MY noble friends, at you I aim,
　　And of myfelf I do complain,
To All bad vices I've been bent,
And yet there's finall amendement;
The devil, the flefh, the world, doth me oppofe,
And are my mighty and my mortal foes;
The devil and flefh doth draw me ftill,
The world on wheels run after with good will;
For that which I the world may juftly call,
I mean the lower glob terreftrial,
Is as the devil and an whore doth pleafe,
Drawn here and there, and every where with eafe;
Thefe that their lives to virtue here do frame,
Are in the world, but yet not of the fame;

Some

Some fuch there are, who neither flefh nor devil,
Can willfully draw on to any evil ;
But for the world, as its the world you fee,
It runs on wheels, and they the palfrey be ;
Which emblem to the reader doth difplay,
The devil, the flefh, do run both fwift away,
The fhrewd infnared world do follow faft,
Till all into perdition's pit be caft.

    Let no man be offended, or think I do him wrong,
In comparing of the gentry unto a fhepherd fwain;
Many ages paft a fhepherd was of fuch dignity,
That gentry he furpaft and beft nobility ;
Cain and Abel brethren were in the firft age of man,
The elder was a hufbander, the younger a fhepherd
      fwain ;
The younger offer'd facrifice to pleafe the high
      Majefty,
The elder was a murderer, given to all villany ;
Some fhepherds paft were kings at laft,
So were never hufbandmen ;
Generals, conquerors, and emperors,
They have been fhepherd fwains :
The renown of a fhepherd fwain
Doth reach unto the fky,
The Charles-Wain fignifies the fame
To the mariners on the fea ;
When you have read and underftood my mind,
I hope your wonted favours I fhall find ;
In fpight of railing bafenefs, whofe lewd tongues
Are Satan's inftruments for flandrous wrongs ;
A thoufand reams of paper it would not contain,
To juftify the worthy fhepherd fwain :
Much hath the Church, our mother, propagated,
By venerable fathers works tranflated :

                      St

St Jerom, Gregory, Ambrofe, Auguftine,
St Bafil, Beries, Cyprian, Conftantine,
Eufebius, Epiphanius, and Origen,
Ignatius, and Lanctantius, (reverend men)
Good Luther, Calvin, learned Zwinglius,
Melancton, Beza, Orcalampadus :
Thefe, and a world more that I can recite,
Their labours would have flept in endlefs night,
But that in paper they preferv'd have been,
And inftruct us to fhun death, hell, and fin.
How fhould we know the change of monarchies,
The Affyrian and the Perfian empires,
Great Alexander's long fmall lafting glory,
Or Rome's high Cæfar, often changing ftory ;
How fhould chronologies of kings be known,
Of either others countries or our own.
Shepherds have been priefts, and fhepherds have
  been kings,
And fhepherds have been emperors, as my mufe
  fings,
Which makes me to compare
The worthy name of Scot
To fhepherds and to fhepherd fwains,
For they flocks and lands have got.
I would have none think thefe I call fhepherd
  fwains,
Is all the name of Scot, and that there's none but
  them,
There's forty-eight that I have fet apart,
All landed gentlemen that live upon their rent ;
And for the fhepherd fwains, I have dedicate them
Each one to a gentleman of that fame name,
All landed gentlemen, that are infeft and feiz'd,
In five month in the year they pay the king his fee;

All befides burgers in city and in town,
That number heretors of refpect and renown:
And for the forty-eight that live upon their rent,
Unto the reader I'm minded to relate,
Becaufe I have not nominate them in fore-time,
I here rehearfe them in my following rhyme.

 Sir Francis Scot of Merigertoun, he hath a good
  eftate,
Although he be but young in years, he is knight
  baronet;
And John Scot of Sinton he is a pretty man,
He outftrips in wifdom any man I ken;
Headfhaw and Burnfoot into the water of Ale,
They are both gentlemen, they dwell in Tiviotdale;
Chappel's a gentleman, Lochthirlfton's another,
 And Gladfwood he's the fame old Gallowfhiels's
  brother;
The laird of Langfhaw him I have no mind to flee,
He is a gentleman and is of kin to me;
The laird of Lochquharret he lives in good report,
So likewife doth the laird of good Hundelfhope;
The laird of Langhope is a very young man,
But the laird of Broadmeadows is both great and
  ftrong;
Into Annandale three lairds of Scots there be,
Heuk, Bagra, and the laird of Gillifbie;
In Efdail-muir there does two lairds remain,
The laird of Johnftoun and laird of Devingtoun:
I'm now for Tiviotdale, if the fates do pleafe,
And not mifs the laird of the Mirrinies;
And the laird of Harwood is a pretty man,
As is any in the fouth of them that I do ken;
The laird of Glack he may not be omitted,
He fold the lands of Gaudilands long ere he got it;
  The

The laird of Alton-crofts I know him well enough,
The laſt lineal male branch that's ſprung of Buck-
    cleugh;
The laird of Whitoch I do him well know,
He is repreſentative of the old family of Headſhaw;
The laird of Caudhouſe he is but a brood,
He is repreſentative to the old houſe of Howfoord;
Three lairds all Scots I muſt exprime,
'Tandlaw, Gallalaw, and Clarilaw's their name;
The laird of Bonraw, a very young man,
The repreſentative of the old family of Sinton;
The laird of Newton he is a gentleman of note,
So is the laird of Alton on Tiviot's burnfoot;
The laird of Brierie-yard I cannot him refer,
Nor yet the laird of Winns, nor laird of Boon-
    chaſter;
Scots-Tarbet and Ardroſs, they are lairds in the
    north,
But ſprung from the loins of Haining in the ſouth;
Bevely and Hallyards I had almoſt forgot,
They deſcended from Lawrence Scot Advocate;
The laird of Carnwath-mill he is a gentleman,
And the repreſentative of the old houſe of Bonni-
    toun;
There's another Bonnitoun into Weſt Louthian,
But I believe he be of Clarkinton's kind;
The laird of Deans-houſes he is a gentleman,
Deſcended from the houſe of Gaudilands;
The laird of Chappel-know I need him not explain,
Through Tiviotdale he's known a gentleman;
The laird of Lies, if that ye woud him knaw;
He is brother to the laird of Clarilaw;
The laird of Clarklands is a gentleman indeed,
From his youth he's been a ſoldier bred;

John

John Scot a quarter mafter, fometime in command,
He married the heretrix of Clarklands;
Betwixt them two was procreat
That French Scots foldier, call'd William Scot:
The laird of Lethen, and the laird of Vogrie,
From the fouth they have their pedigree.
Here's an hundred and ten heretors of credit and
   renown,
All gentlemen, befides burgeffes in towns,
And for every one of thefe five fcore,
Of the worthy name of Scot there's above a hun-
   dred more,
Which the number of ten thoufand doth exceed,
In the forreft and Tiviotdale on the fouth fide of
   Tweed,
All of one kindred into that country fide;
I mean not the fpacious nation long and wide,
But from one root thefe worthy branches fprang
Like Jacob's feed, when they to Egypt came:
I wifh Apollo from great Atlas mountain,
Affift them with his grace to fulfil their fountain;
That virtue, love, and grace, amongft them ever
   grow,
And that their fountain ftill may overflow.
Like trees in wood, fome great, fome fmall,
So is our heretors, yet gentlemen all;
There's many moe that to me is not known,
For never a man to me a fingle one has fhown,
If I fhould pick from burgh or ftot,
Landed gentlemen of the name of Scot,
Although it unto me would be a cumber,
Yet I could have added forty to the number;
An hundred heritors of one name,
The like in Scotland I've not feen.
       When

When Walter Earl of Buccleugh he did to Hol-
　　land wain,
There went with him a hundred gentlemen of that
　　name,
For befides private foldiers, thefe did gang;
But friends and relations to attend his own perfon;
If he had been alive in the bygone troublefome
　　time,
He might have rais'd a thoufand, all of his own
　　name;
And never a man been threatened by force,
But all volunteers for foot and horfe;
My verfe is honeft, true, feemly and mild,
My mufe fhall wade through dirt and not be fil'd;
The fun on loathfome dunghills fhines as well,
As on fair flowers that have a fragrant fmell;
The air, by which we live, doth every where
Breathe ftill alike upon the rich and poor;
The fea bears many an old defpifed fhip,
Yet on the fea the beft fhip doth but float;
And earth allows to call his fcatter'd brood,
Food, clothes, and lodging, either good or bad;
Yet fun, air, fea and earth, thinks it difgrace,
For any bounty which they give the bafe;
Even fo my mufe, free from all foul intents,
Doth take example from the elements:
Yet will I not my fenfe or meaning mar,
With terms obfcure, nor phrafes fetcht from far,
Nor will I any way equivocate,
With words fophiftical or intricate;
Small eloquence men muft expect from me,
My fchollarfhip will name things as they be;
I may fet out this little book indeed,
Yet cannot write and little thing can read:
　　　　　　　　　　　　　　　　And

And now I fear I have done wrong,
In calling my friends shepherd swains,
So many sorts of shepherds constantly do grow,
That where there is no shepherds it is hard to know;
Cast but your eyes upon the man of Rome,
That stiles himself the head of Christendom,
Christ's universal vicar and vicegerent,
In whom fools think the truth is inherent,
That he can souls to heaven or hell prefer,
And being full of errors cannot err ;
Although his witchcraft a thousand have imbrac'd,
Yet he'll be call'd the Lieutenant to Christ,
Who by that false Conventicle of Trent,
Made laws that neither God nor good men meant,
Commanding worshipping of stones and stocks,
Of reliques, dead mens bones, and senseless blocks ;
From which adultery, painted adulation,
Men worse than stock or block must seek salvation.
Great Julius Cæsar was so free and common,
And call'd a husband unto every woman;
Proculus, emperor (the story says),
Deflower'd an hundred maids in fifteen days :
If all be true that poets use to write,
Hercules lay with fifty in one night ;
When Heliogabulus Rome's scepter sway'd,
And all the world his lawless laws obey'd,
He in his court caus'd stews be made,
Whereas (*cum privilegio*) whores did trade,
He invited two and twenty of his friends,
And kindly to each one a whore he lends ;
To set whores free that then in bondage lay,
A mighty mass of money he did pay ;
He in one day gave to each whore in Rome
A ducat, a large and ill bestowed sum ;

He

He made orations unto whores, and faid,
They were his foldiers, his defence and aid ;
And in his fpeech he fhew'd his wits acute,
Of fundry forms of bawdry to difpute ;
And after giving unto every whore,
For liftening to his tale three ducats more ;
With pardon unto all and liberty,
That would be whores within his monarchy ;
And yearly penfions he freely gave,
To keep a regiment of whores moft brave ;
And oft he had, when he in progrefs went,
Of whores, bawds, pandreffes, fuch a rablement,
Six hundred waggons, as hiftories reports,
Attended only by thofe brave conforts :
This was a royal whore-mafter indeed,
A fpecial benefactor in their need ;
But none fince Heliogabulus deceaft,
I think the world with whores is fo increaft,
That if it had an emperor as mad,
He might have twice fo many as he had.
Here I leave whores and whore-mafters,
Unto the man of Rome ;
And to the worthy fhepherd fwain,
I prefently return.
　Becaufe I know and prefently maintain,
That he that laboureth to be a worthy man,
May with a better confcience fleep in bed,
Than with the gout and gravel as I'm fped,
Yet to keep my health from falling to decay,
When I am moft tormented, I terrifie ;
A thoufand times it is more pains than dead,
I'm fure it by antiquity hath ftood,
Since the world's drowning univerfal flood :
　　　　　　　Though

Though my wits be like my purse, but bare,
With poets I dare not compare,
Yet to dite verse, provided that they be,
No better skill'd in scholarship than me,
' And then come on as many as you will.
' And for a wager, I'll verse with them still;
Myself I liken to an untun'd viol,
For like a viol I'm in a case,
And whoso of my fortune makes a trial,
Shall like to me be strung and tuned base;
And treble troubles he shall never want:
But here's the period of my mischiefs all,
Though base and treble fortune did me grant,
And means, but yet alas it is too scant;
Yet to make up the music, I'll venture a fall,
To the tenor in the Carset town-hall:
A poet rightly may be termed fit
An abstract or epitome of wit,
Or like a lute, that other pleasures breed,
Are sweet and strong their curious eyes to feed,
That scornfully distaste it, yet it's known,
It makes the hearers sport, but itself none:
A poet's like a taper burnt by night,
That wastes itself in giving others light;
A poet's the most fool beneath the skies,,
He spends his wit in making others wise;
Who, when they should their thankfulness return,
They pay him with disdain, contempt and scorn,
An independant is like a poet's purse;
For both do hate the cross, what cross is worse?
His holy hymns, and psalms for confolation,
For reprehension, and for contemplation;
And finally to show us our salvation,

The

The prophet Amos, unto whom the Lord
Reveal'd the facred fecrets of his word,
God rais'd him from the fheep-folds to foretell,
What plagues fhall fall in finful Ifrael;
True patience, pattern prince of his afflictions,
Moft mighty tamer of his imperfections,
Whofe guard was God, whofe guid's the Holy Ghoft,
Bleft in his wealth, of whom fheep was the moft;
Juft Job's laft riches doubled was again,
Who liv'd belov'd of God, admir'd of men:
The firft of happy tidings on the earth,
Of our all only bleffed Saviour's birth;
The glorious angels to the fhepherds told,
As Luke the Evangelift doth unfold.
And, fhould my verfe a little but decline,
To human ftories, and leave divine;
There are fome mighty princes I can name,
Whofe breeding at the firft from fhepherds came;
Rome's founder Romulus was bred and fed
'Mongft fhepherds, where his youthful days he led;
The Perfian monarch Cyrus he did pafs
His youth with fhepherds, and a fhepherd was;
The terror of the world, that famous man,
Who conquer'd kings, and over kingdoms ran,
His ftile was, as fome hiftories do repeat,
The Scythian fhepherd, Tamerlane the Great;
'Tis fuch a title of preheminence,
Of reverence, and fuch high magnificence;
That David who fo well his words did frame,
Did call our great Creator by that name;
Our bleft redeemer, God's eternal fon,
Whofe only merits our falvation won,
He did the harmlefs name of fhepherd take.

X   Apollo

Apollo father of the fifters nine,
I crave thee, and infpire this mufe of mine;
Thou that thy golden glory didft lay by,
As Ovid doth relate moft wittily,
And in a fhepherd's fhape didft deign to keep,
Thy loves beloved Adamus fheep;
And rural Pan thy help I do intreat,
That to the life thy praife I may repeat';
Of the contented life, and mighty ftocks,
Are happy fhepherds, and their harmlefs flocks;
But better thoughts my errors do controul,
For an offence moft negligent and foul,
In this involving like an heathen man;
Help helplefs from Apollo, or from Pan;
When as the fubject which I have in hand,
Is almoft infinite, as ftars, or fand;
Grac'd with antiquity upon record,
In the eternal never-failing word;
There 'tis ingraven, true and manifeft,
That fheep and fhepherds were both beft and bleft;
I therefore invocate the gracious aid,
Of him whofe mighty hand hath all things made;
I Ifrael's great fhepherd humbly crave,
That his affur'd affiftance I may have;
That my unlearned mufe no verfe compile,
Which may be impious, profane, or vile;
And though, through ignorance, or negligence,
My poor intention fall into offence,
I do implore that boundlefs grace of his,
Not ftrictly to regard what is amifs;
But unto me belongeth all the blame,
And all the glory be unto his name;
Yet as my book is verfe, fo men may know,
I might fome fictions and allufions fhow:

Some

Some ſhreds or remnants, reliques, or ſome ſcrapes,
The muſes may inſpire me with perhaps,
Which taken literally, as't lyes may ſeem,
And ſo miſunderſtanding may miſdeem.
Of ſheep therefore before to work I fall,
To ſhow the ſhepherds firſt original;
Theſe that the beſt records will read and mark,
Shall find juſt Abel was a patriarch,
Our father Adam's ſecond ſon a prince,
As great as any man begotten ſince;
And in his function he a ſhepherd was,
And ſo his mortal pilgrimage did paſs;
And in the ſacred text it is compil'd,
That he that's father of the faithful ſtil'd,
Did as a ſhepherd live upon th' increaſe
Of ſheep, until his days on earth did ceaſe;
And in theſe times it was apparent then,
Abram and Abel both were noble men;
The one obtain'd the title righteouſly,
For his unfeigned ſerving the moſt high;
He firſt did offer ſheep, which on record,
Was ſacrifice accepted of the Lord;
He was, before the infant world was ripe,
The church's figure, and our Saviour's type;
A murdered martyr, who, for ſerving God,
Did firſt of all feel perſecution's rod;
And Abram was in account ſo great,
Abimelech his friendſhip did intreat,
Faith's patern, and obedience ſample he,
Like ſtars, or ſand, was in proſperity,
In him the nations of the earth were bleſt,
And now his boſom figures heavenly reſt;
His ſheep almoſt paſt numbring multiplied,
And when as he thought Iſaac ſhould have died,

X 2   Then

Then by the Almighty's mercies, love, and grace,
A sheep from out the bush supplied the place ;
Lot was a shepherd, Abram's brother son,
And such great favour from his God he won,
That Sodom could not be consum'd with fire,
Till he and his did out of it retire ;
They felt no vengeance for their foul offence,
Till righteous Lot was quite departed hence ;
And Jacob, as the Holy Ghost doth tell,
Who afterward was called Israel,
Who wrestled with his God, and to his fame
Obtain'd a name, and blessing for the same ;
He under Laban was a shepherd long,
And suffer'd from him much ungrateful wrong ;
For Rachel and Leah he did bear,
The yoke of servitude full twenty year :
He was a patriarch, a prince of might,
Whose wealth in sheep was almost infinite ;
His twice six sons, as holy writ describes,
Who were the famous fathers of twelve tribes,
Were for the most part shepherds, and such men,
Whose like the world shall ne'er contain again ;
Young Joseph 'monst the rest especially,
A constant mirror of true chastity,
Who was in his afflictions of behaviour
A mortal type of his immortal Saviour,
And truth his mother Rachel doth exprefs,
To be her father Laban's shepherdefs.
Meek Mofes whom the Lord of Hosts did call,
To lead his people out of Egypt's thrall,
Whose power was so much as none before,
Or since his time hath any man's been more,
Within the sacred text it plainly appears,
That he was Jethro's shepherd twenty years ;

Heroic

Heroic David, Jeffe's youngeft fon,
Whofe acts immortal memory hath won,
Whofe valiant vigour did in pieces tear
A furious lion and a ravenous bear,
Who, arm'd with faith and fortitude alone,
Slew great Goliah with a flinging ftone ;
Whofe victories the people fang moft plain,
Saul hath a thoufand, he ten thoufand flain,
He from the fheep-fold came to be a king,
Whofe fame for ever through the world fhall ring;
He was another type of that Moft High,
That was, and is, and evermore fhall be,
For our protection and his mercies fake.
Thofe that will read the facred text, and look
With diligence throughout that heavenly book,
Shall find the Minifters have epithets,
And named angels, ftewards, watchmen, lights,
All builders, hufbandmen, and ftars that fhine,
Inflamed with the light that is divine,
And with thefe names within that book compil'd,
They with the ftile of fhepherds are inftil'd ;
Thus God the feer and fon the fcriptures call,
Both fhepherds myftical and literal ;
And by fimilitudes comparing, do
All kings and church-men bear that title too.
Wife and unfcrutable, omnifcient,
Eternal, gracious, and omnipotent,
In love, in juftice, mercy, and in might,
In honour, power, and glory infinite,
In works, in words, in every attribute ;
Almighty, all-commanding, abfolute,
For whofo notes the letters of the name,
Jehovah, fhall perceive within the fame,

The

The vowels of all tongues ~   ~ed be,
So hath no name, that c'~   ~med but He.
And I have heard fome fc~~~~~ make relation,
That H is but a breathing afpiration,
A letter that may be left out and fpared,
Whereby is clearly to our fight declared,
That great Jehovah may be written true,
With only vowels, a, e, i, o, u.
And that there is no word but this,
That hath them alone, but only this,
So that the heaven, with all the mighty hoft
Of creatures there, earth, fea, or any coaft,
Or climate, any fifh, or fowl, or beaft,
Or any of his works, the moft and leaft,
Or thoughts, or words, or writing with the pen,
Or deeds that are accomplifhed by men,
But have fome of thefe letters in them all,
And God alone hath all in general :
By which we fee, according to his will,
He is in all things, and does all things fill ;
And all things faid or done he hath ordain'd,
Some part of his great name's therein contain'd :
All future, prefent, and all paft things feeing ;
In him we live, and move, and have our being ;
Almighty, all, and all in every where,
Eternal, in whom change cannot appear ;
Immortal, who made all things mortal elfe,
Omnipotent, whofe power all power excels ;
United three in one, and one in three,
Jehovah, unto whom all glory be.
 Befides the learned poets of all times,
Have chanted out their praife in pleafant rhimes,
The harmlefs lives of rural fhepherd fwains,
And beauteous fhepherdeffes on the plains,

                                        In

In odes, in roundelays, and madrigals,
In fonnets, and in well-penn'd poft'rals,
They have recorded moft delightfully
Their loves, their fortunes, and felicity ;
And fure, if in this low terreftrial round,
Plain honeft happinefs is to be found,
It with the fhepherds is remaining ftill,
Becaufe they have leaft power to do ill ;
And whilft they on their feeding flocks attend,
They have the leaft occafions to offend ;
Ambition, pomp, and hell-begotten pride,
And damned adulation they deride,
The complemental flatt'ry of kings courts
Is never intermixed with their fports ;
They feldom envy at each others ftate,
Their love and fear is God's, the devil's their hate;
In weighty bufinefs they do not mar or make,
And curfed bribes they neither give nor take ;
They are not guilty as fome great men are,
To undo their merchant and embroiderer ;
Nor is't a fhepherd's trade by night or day,
To fwear themfelves and never pay ;
He's no State-ploting Machivilian ;
Or project-monger Monopolitan ;
He hath no tricks or wiles to circumvent,
Nor fears he when there comes a parliament ;
He never wears a cap, nor bends his knee,
To feed contention with an advocate's fee ;
He wants the art to cog, cheat, fwear, and lie,
Nor fears the gallows nor the pillory,
Nor cares he if great men be fools or wife,
If honour fall, and bafe difhonour rife ;

                                        Let

Let fortune's mounted minions fink or fwim,
He never breaks his brains, all's one to him:
He's free from fearful curfes of the poor,
And lives and dies content with lefs or more.
He doth not wafte the time as many ufe,
His good Creator's creatures to abufe,
In drinking fuch ungodly healths to fome,
The verieft canker-worms in Chriftendom;
My Lord Ambition, and my Lady Pride,
Shall with this quaffing not be magnified,
Nor for their fakes fhall he caroufe and feaft,
Until from man he turn worfe than a beaft;
Whereby he 'fcapes vain oaths and blafphemy,
And furfeits fruits of drunken gluttony;
He 'fcapes occafion unto luft's pretence,
And fo efcapes the pox by confequence;
Thus doth he hate the parator and procter,
The apothecary, chirurgeon and doctor,
Whereby he this prerogative may have,
To hold while he be laid into his grave;
Whilft many that his betters far have been,
Will very hardly hold the laying in:
Crook, blanket, terkit, tarrier-like, call'd Croufe,
Shall breed no jars into the Parliament-houfe.
Thus fhepherds live, and thus they end their lives,
Adorn'd and grac'd with thefe prerogatives,
And when he dies, he leaves no wrangling heirs,
To law, till all be fpent, and nothing theirs,
Peace and tranquillity was all his life,
And dead, his goods fhall breed no caufe of ftrife.
Thus fhepherds have no places, means or times,
To fall into thefe hell-deferving crimes,

Which

Which courtiers, lawyers, tradefmen, men of arms,
Commit unto their fouls and bodies harms.
　　And from the fhepherds now I turn my ftile,
To fundry forts of fheep another while;
The lambs that in the Jew's paffover died,
Were figures of the Lamb that's crucified;
And Ifaiah doth compare our heavenly food
To a fheep, which dumb before the fhearer ftood,
Whofe death and merits did this title win,
The Lamb of God, which freed the world from fin;
The anagram of Lamb is blame and blame,
And Chrift the Lamb upon him took our blame;
His precious blood God's heavy wrath did calm,
'Twas the only balm for fin, to cure the fame;
All power and praife and glory be therefore
Afcribed to the Lamb for evermore:
And in the fourfcore pfalm we read,
That like a flock our God doth Jofeph lead;
Again of us he fuch account doth keep,
That of his pafture we are called fheep;
And every day we do confefs almoft,
That we have err'd and ftray'd like fheep that's loft;
Our Saviour that hath bought our fouls fo dear,
Hath faid his fheep his voice will only hear;
And thrice did Chrift unto St Peter call,
In which he fpake to his difciples all,
If ye do love me, feed my fheep, (quoth he)
And feed my lambs if ye love me;
Moreover in the final judgement day,
There is the right hand, and the left hand way,
Whereas the fheep he to himfelf doth gather,
With faying, Come, ye bleffed of my father, &c,

Y　　　　　　　　　　　And

And to the goats in his confuming ire,
He fays depart to everlafting fire.
Thus our redeemer and his whole elect,
The name of fheep had ever in refpect,
And the comparifon holds reference,
To profit and to harmlefs innocence;
For of all beafts that ever were or are,
None can for goodnefs with a fheep compare;
Indeed for bone and burden I muft grant,
He's much inferior to the elephant;
The dromedary, camel, horfe, and afs,
For load and carriage doth the fheep furpafs;
Strong Taurus, Eunuch's fon, the labouring ox,
The ftately ftag, the bobtail'd crafty fox;
Thefe, and all rav'nous beafts of prey muft yield,
Unto the fheep the honour of the field;
I could recount the names of many more,
The lion, unicorn, the bear, and boar,
The wolf, the tyger, the rhinoceros,
The leopard, and a number more I wot;
But all thefe greedy beafts great Ovid's pen,
Calls metamorphos'd into men;
For beaft to beaft afford more confcience can,
And much lefs cruelty than man to man;
I'll therefore let fuch beafts be as they be,
For fear they kick and fnarl at me.
Unto the fheep again my mufe doth flee,
For honeft fafety and commoditie,
He with his flefh and fleece doth cleed and feed,
All languages and nations, good and bad.
What can it more than die, that we may live,
And ev'ry year to us a liv'ry give;

'Tis such a bounty, and the charge so deep,
That nothing can defray the charge but sheep;
For, should the world want sheep but five whole year,
Ten thousand millions would want cloths to wear:
And wer't not for the flesh of this kind beast,
The world might fast when it doth often feast;
There's nothing doth unto a sheep pertain,
But 'tis for man's commodity and gain;
For men to men so much untrusty are,
To lie, to cozen, to foreswear and swear,
That oaths, and passing words, and joining hands,
Is like assurance written in the sands;
To make men keep their words, and in end this
The silly sheep-skin turn'd to parchment is;
There's many a wealthy man whose whole estate
Lies more in parchment than in coin or plate,
Indentures, leafes, evidences, wills,
Bonds, contracts, records. obligations, bills,
With these, although the sheep-skin be but weak,
It binds men strongly that they dare not break:
But if a man eats spiders now and then,
The oil of parchment cures him oft again,
And what rare stuffs which in the world are fram'd
Can be in value like to parchment nam'd?
The richest cloth of gold that can be found,
A yard of it was ne'er worth five hundred pound;
And I have seen two foot of sheep-skin drest,
Which have been worth ten thousand pound at least;
A piece of parchment well with ink laid o'er,
Helps many gallant to a starving power;
Into the merchant it some faith doth strike,
It gives the silkman hope of no dislike;

　　　　　　The

The taylor it with charity affails,
It thrufts him laft betwixt his bill and vails;
And by thefe means a piece of parchment can
Patch up and make a gull a gentleman:
The nature of it very ftrange I find,
It's much like phyfic it can loofe and bind;
It's one man's freedom and another's lofs,
And like the Pope it doth both bind and loofe;
And as the ram and ewe doth fructifie,
And ev'ry year a lamb doth multiply,
So doth a fheep-fkin bond make money breed,
And procreat, as feed doth fpring from feed.
  Thus is a fheep-fkin prov'd the only tye,
And ftay whereon a world of men rely,
' Which holds a crew of earth-worms in more awe,
' Than both the tables of the facred law;
Paft number I could functions name,
Who as it's parchment live upon the fame;
But it's fufficient this fmall homely touch;
Should more be writ, my book would fwell too
    much.
Now for the ram, the ewe, the lamb and weather,
I'll touch their fkins as they are touch'd to leather;
And made in purfes, pouches, laces, ftrings,
Gloves, points, books, covers, and ten thoufand
    things;
And many tradefmen live and thrive thereby,
Which if I would I more could amplify;
Their guts ferve inftruments, which fweetly found,
Their dung is beft to make moft fruitful ground,
Their hoofs burnt will moft venomous ferpents kill,
Their grated horns are good for poifon ftill,
                    Their

Their milk makes cheefe that has no fellow,
The beft that's made in Etrick or in Yarrow;
Their feet for the healthy or the fick,
Dreft as they fhould be, are good meat to pick;
The cook and butcher with the joints do gain,
And poor folks eat the gedder, head, and brain;
And though all wife mens judgements will allow,
A fheep to be much leffer than a cow.
Now for the honour of the valiant ram,
If I were learn'd more treble than I am,
Yet could I not fufficiently exprefs,
His wondrous worth and excellent worthinefs;
For by aftronomers it is verified,
How that the ram in heaven is ftylified,
And of the twelve is plac'd head fign of all,
Where Sol keeps firft his equinoctial;
For having with the Bull drunk April fhowers,
And with the Twins doth deck the earth with
    flowers,
And fcorch'd the Crab in June with burning
    beams,
Made July's Lion chaff with fiery gleams,
In Auguft folace to the Virgin given,
With balance in September made time even,
October Scorpion with declining courfe,
And paffing by November's Archers force;
Then having paft December's frozen gate,
He next to Janus wat'ry fign doth float,
He to the Lentil fign in February,
And fo bright Phœbus ends his years fligarie;
Then to the Ram in March in his carrier,
He mounts, on which this fonnet's written here.

Now

Now cheerful Sol, in his illuftrious car,
To glade the earth his journey 'gins to take,
And now his glorious beams he doth unbar,
While's abfence marr'd, his prefence now doth
       make ;
Now he earth's weeping 'gins to dry,
With Eolus breath and his bright heavenly heat,
March-duft like clouds through air doth march and
       fly,
And feeming trees and plants now life doth get ;
Thus when the world's eye-dazler takes his time,
At the celeftial Ram then winter's done,
And then dame nature doth her livery fpin,
Of flowers and fruits, which all the earth puts on ;
Thus when Apollo doth to Aries come,
The earth is freed from winter's martyrdom.

   Thus have I prov'd the Ram a lucky fign,
Wherein fun, earth, and heaven, and air combine,
To have their univerfal comfort harl'd,
Upon the face of our decaying world.
With twelve figns each man's body is governed,
And Aries of the Ram doth rule the head ;
Then are the judgements foolifh, fond and bafe,
That take the name of ram-head in difgrace ;
'Tis honour for the head to have the name,
Derived from the ram that rules the fame ;
' And that the ram doth rule the head I know,
' For ev'ry almanack the fame doth fhow.

   From whence fuch men may gather this relief,
That though a ram-head may be caufe of grief ;
Yet nature hath this remedy found out,
They fhould have lion's hearts to bear it out ;
                 And

And to defend and keep the head from harm,
The anagram of ram I find is arm ;
Thus is a ram-head arm'd againft all fear,
He needs no helmet, nor no head-piece wear ;
To fpeak more in the plural number rams,
It yields fignific war-like anagrams ;
The ram is Mars, Mars is the god of war,
And ram is arms, arms war's munitions are ;
And from the fierce encounters which they make,
Our tilts and turneys did beginning take ;
For as the rams retire, and meet with rage,
So men do in their warlike equipage ;
And long ere powder from hell's damn'd den,
Was monftroufly produc'd to murder men,
The ram, an engine call'd a ram did teach,
To batter down a wall, or make a breach ;
And now fome places of defence 'gainft fhot,
Have from the ram the name of rampiers got ;
Firft warlike trumpets that I e'er heard nam'd,
At Jericho, were all of ram-horns fram'd,
For at the ram-horn trumpets fearful blaft,
Their curled walls were fuddenly down caft :
Thus is the ram with many virtues ftor'd,
And was in Egypt for a god ador'd ;
And, like a captain he the flock doth lead,
As fits their general, their prince and head.

   Thus have I prov'd a fheep a beaft of price,
Clean, and reputed fit for facrifice ;
And fleeping, waking, early, or elfe late,
It ftill doth chew the cud and ruminate :
Of all beafts in the world's circumference,
For meeknefs, profit, and for innocence,

                        I have

I have approv'd a sheep most excellent,
That with least cost gives most content ;
There's such instinct of nature in the lamb,
By bleating, it 'mongst thousands knows the dame.
For which the name of agnofcendo knowing,
Is given to a lamb, its knowledge showing.
 And now from solid profe I will abstain,
To pleasant poetry, and mirth again ;
The fables of the golden fleece began,
Becaufe sheep wool yields store of gold to men ;
For he that hath great store of woolly fleeces,
May when he please have store of golden pieces :
Thus many a poor man dying hath left a son,
That hath transform'd the fleece to gold like Jafon.
And here's a myftery profound and deep,
There's fundry forts of mutton are no sheep ;
Lac'd mutton, which let out themfelves to hire,
Like hackneys, will be fir'd before they tire ;
The man, or men which for fuch mutton hungers
Are, by their corporations, mutton-mungers,
Which is a brother-hood fo large and great,
That, if they had a hall, I would intreat
To be their clerk or keeper of accounts,
To shew them unto what their charge amounts.
My brain in numbring then would grow fo quick,
I should be mafter of arithmetic ;
All states, degrees, and trades, both bad and good,
Afford fome members of this brother-hood ;
Great therefore, then muft be their multitude,
When every man may to the trade intrude,
It is no freedom, yet thefe men are free ;
No favers, but moft liberal fpenders be ;

For

For this is one thing that doth them bewitch,
That by their trading they wax seldom rich;
The value of his mutton so set forth,
The flesh doth cost more than the broth is worth;
They all are ewes, yet are exceeding ramish,
And will be dainty fed, who ever famish;
Nor are they marked for any man, or no man,
As mine, or thine, but every man is common;
Fine heads, and necks, and breasts they yield some
        store,
But scarcely one good liver in ninescore;
The liver being bad, it's understood,
The veins are fill'd with putrified blood,
Which makes them subject to the scab, and then
They prove most dangerous diets unto men;
And then the proverb proves no ly or mock,
One scabbed sheep's enough to spoil a flock.
But yet, for all this, there's many a gull,
Loves mutton well, dips not his bread i' th' wool;
And were a man put to his choice to keep,
'Tis said a shrew is better than a sheep;
But if a man be yoked with such an ewe,
She may be both a scabbed sheep and shrew;
And he that is so macht't, his life may well
Be compared unto an earthly hell.
But of my theme which I wrote of before,
I at this mutton must have one cut more;
These kind of sheep have all the world o'ergrown,
And seldom do wear fleeces of their own;
For they from sundry men their pellets can pull,
Whereby they keep themselves as warm as wool;
Besides in colours, and in shapes they wear,
Quite from all profitable sheep contrair;

Z   White,

White, black, green, tawny, purple, red, and blue,
Beyond the rain-bow, for the change of hue;
Came foon like an alteration,
But that bare air they cannot live upon;
The moon's mutation not more manifold,
Silk, velvet, tiffue, cloth, and cloth of gold.
Thefe are the fheep that golden fleeces wear,
Who robe themfelves with others wool or hair;
And it may be 'twas fuch a beaft and fleece,
Which Jafon brought from Colchos into Greece;
Were it no more but fo I dare be bold
To think the land doth many Jafon's hold,
Who never durft to pafs a dangerous wave,
Yet may with eafe fuch golden fleeces have.
Too much of one thing is good for nothing, they
    fay,
I'll therefore take this needlefs difh away;
For fhould I too much of lac'd mutton write,
I may o'ercome my reader's ftomach quite;
Once more unto the good fheep I'll retire,
And fo my book fhall to it's end expire;
Although it be not found in ancient writers,
I find all mutton-eaters are fheep-biters;
And in fome places, I have heard and feen,
That currifh fheep-biters they have hanged been;
'If any kind of tyke fhould fnarl or whinne,
'Or bite or worry this poor fheep of mine,
'Why? Let them bark, or bite, and fpend their
    breath,
'I'll never wifh them a fheep-biter's death;
My fheep fhould have them know their innocence,
Shall live in fpight of their malevolence;
                    I wifh

I wifh they keep themfelves and me from pain,
And bite fuch fheep, as cannot bite again;
For if they fnap at mine, I have a tongue,
That like a trufty dog fhall bite again;
And in conclufion, this I humbly crave,
That every one the honefty may have,
That when our frail mortality is paft,
We may be the good fhepherd's fheep at laft.
When all things were as wrapt in fable night,
And ebon'd darknefs muffled up the night,
When neither fun, nor moon, nor ftars had fhin'd,
And when no fire, no water, earth, nor wind,
No fummer, autumn, winter, nor no fpring,
No bird, beaft, fifh, nor any creeping thing,
When there was neither time, nor place, nor fpace,
And filence did the Chaos round embrace;
Then did the Arch-work-mafter of us all,
Create this maffy univerfal ball,
And with his mighty word brought all to pafs,
Saying, but let there be, and done it was;
Let there be day, night, water, earth, herbs, trees,
Let there be fun, moon, ftars, fifh, fowl that flies,
Beaft of the field; he faid, let there be;
All things were created, as we may fee.
Thus every fenfible and fenflefs thing,
The high Creator's word to pafs did bring;
And as in viewing of his works he ftood,
He faid, that all things were exceeding good:
Thus having finifh'd feas, and earth, and fkies,
Abundantly with all varieties,
Like a magnificent and fumptuous feaft,
To th' entertainment of fome welcome gueft,

When beafts, and birds, and every living creature,
And the earth's fruits did multiply by nature;
Then did the eternal Trinity betake
Itfelf to council, and faid, let us make,
Not let there be, as unto all things elfe,
But let us make man that the reft excells;
According to our image, let us make
Man; and then the Almighty red earth did take,
With which he formed Adam every limb,
And having made him, breathed life in him.
Lo thus the firft man never was a child,
No way with fin original defil'd;
But with high fuper-natural underftanding,
He over all the world had fole commanding;
Yet though to him the regency was given
As earth's lieutenant to the God of heaven,
Though he commanded all created things,
As deputy under the king of kings,
Though he fo highly there was dignified,
To humble him, not to be puft with pride;
He could not brag nor boaft of high-born birth,
For he was formed out of flime and earth;
No beaft, fifh, worm, fowl, herb, wood, ftone, tree,
But are of a more ancient houfe than he;
For they were made before him, which prove this,
That their antiquity is more than his.
Thus both himfelf, and his beloved fpoufe,
Are by creation of the younger houfe;
And whilft they live in perfect holinefs,
Their richeft garments were bare nakednefs,
True innocence were their chiefeft weeds;
For righteoufnefs no mafk or vizard needs;

                        The

The royalist robes that our first parents had,
Was a free conscience with uprightness clad;
They needed not to shift, the clothes they wore
Was nakedness, and they desir'd no more;
Untill at last, that hell-polluting sin,
With disobedience fold their soul within;
And having lost their holiest perfection
They held their nakedness in imperfection;
Then being both asham'd, they both did frame,
Garments as weeds of their deserved shame;
Thus when as sin had brought God's curse on man,
Then shame to make apparel first began;
Ere men had sin'd most plain it does appear,
He neither did, nor needed cause men swear;
For his apparel did at first begin,
To be the robes of penance for his sin;
Thus all the brood of Adam, and of Eve,
The true use of apparel may perceive;
That they are liveries, badges unto all,
Of our sins, and our parents woeful fall;
Then more than mad the mad-brain'd people be,
Or else they see, and will not seem to see,
The same robes of pride that makes them swell,
Are tokens that our best deserts are hell,
Much like unto a traitor to his king,
Which would his country into destruction bring,
Whose treacheries being prov'd apparently,
He by the law is justly judg'd to die;
And when he looks for his deserved death,
A pardon comes, and gives him longer breath,
I think this man most madly would appear,
That would a halter in a glory wear,

Of

Of life to be quite dif-inherited;
But if he fhould vain glorioufly perfift,
To make a rope of filk, or golden twift,
And wear, it's a more honourable fhow
Of his rebellion than coarfe hemp or tow;
Might not men juftly fay he were an afs,
Triumphing that he once a villain was,
And that he wears an halter for the nonce,
In pride that he deferv'd a hanging once.
Such with our heavenly father is the cafe,
Of our firft parents, and their fruitful race;
Apparel is the miferable fign,
That we are traitors to our Lord divine,
And we like rebels ftill moft pride do take,
In that which ftill moft humble fhould us make;
Apparel is the prifon for our fin,
Which moft fhould fhame, yet moft we glory in;
Apparel is the fheet of fhame, as it were;
For man apparel never did receive,
Till he eternal death deferv'd to have:
How vain it is for man, a clod of earth,
To boaft of his progeny or birth,
Becaufe perhaps his anceftors were good,
And fprung from royal or from noble blood;
Where virtues worth did in their minds inherit,
They enjoy'd their honour by defert and merit.
Great Alexander, king of Macedon,
Difdain'd to be his father Philip's fon,
But he from Jupiter would be defcended,
And as a god be honour'd and attended;
Yet when at Babylon he prov'd but a man,
His god-head ended foolifh as't began;

There

There was in Sicily a proud phyſician,
Menocrates, and he through high ambition,
To be a god himſelf would needs prefer,
And would forſooth be deem'd Jupiter;
King Dionyſius making a great feaſt,
The fool god diſguis'd to be a great beaſt;
Who by himſelf was at a table plac'd,
Becauſe as god he ſhould the more be grac'd;
The other gueſts themſelves did feed and fill,
He at an empty table ſtill ſat ſtill;
At laſt with humble low Sir Reverence,
A fellow came with fire and frankincenſe,
And offered to his god-ſhip, ſaying then,
Perfumes were fit for gods, and meat for men;
The god in anger raiſe incontinent,
Who laughed, and in hunger homeward went.
The Roman Emperor Domitian
Would be a god, was murdered by a man.
Caligula would be a god of wonders,
And counterfeit the lightening and the thunders,
Yet every real heavenly thunder crack,
This cateif in ſuch fear and terror ſtrake,
That he would quake, and ſhake, and hide his
        head
In any hole, or underneath his bed;
And when this godleſs god had many ſlain,
A Plebeian daſht out his ungodly brain:
And thus the Almighty ſtill againſt pride doth
        frown,
And caſts ambition headlong tumbling down.
Great Pompey would be all the world's ſuperior,
And Cæſar unto none would be inferior;

                                    But

But as they both did live ambitiously,
So both of them untimeous deaths did die:
The one in Egypt had his final fall,
The other murdered in the capital.
A number more examples are beside,
Which shows the miserable fall of pride;
For pride of state, birth, wisdom, beauty, strength,
And pride in any thing will fall at length;
But to be proud of garments that we wear,
Is the most foolish pride a heart can bear;
Know that of thine own thou doth possess,
Nothing but sin and woeful wretchedness;
A Christian's pride should only be in this,
When he can say, that God his father is;
When grace and mercy well applied, afford
To make him brother unto Christ his Lord;
When he unto the Holy Ghost can say,
Thou art my schoolmaster whom I will obey.
When he can call the saints his fellows, and
Say to the angels, for my guard you stand:
This is a laudable and christian pride,
To know Christ and to know him crucified;
This is that meek ambition low aspiring,
Which all men should be earnest in desiring:
Thus to be proudly humble is the thing,
Which will us to the state of glory bring;
But yet beware of pride hypocritical,
For pride in every thing will have a fall;
A lofty mind with lowly cap on knee,
Is humble pride and meek hypocrisie;
As a great ship ill suited with small sail,
A Judas mean'd all mischief, cry'd all hail;

Like

Like the humility of Abfalom,
That fort of pride much dnager waits upon;
They are the counterfeit, God fave you, Sirs,
That have their flatteries in particulars,
That courteoufly can hide their own intents,
Under varieties of complements;
Thefe vipers bend the knee, and kifs the hand,
And fwear, fweet Sir, I am at your command;
And proudly make humility a fcrew,
To wring themfelves into opinion's view:
Thus pride is hateful, dangerous and vile,
And fhall itfelf at laft itfelf beguile:
Thus pride is deadly fin, and fin brings fhame,
Which here I leave to hell from whence it came.

SINCE the water of Ail Scots they are all chang'd
        and gone,
Except brave Whitflade and Hardin,
And Satchels his eftate is gone,
Except his poor defignation,
Which never no man fhall poffefs,
Except a Scot defigned Satchels.
        Therefore begone my book, ftretch forth thy
            wings and fly,
Amongft the nobles and gentility:
Thou'rt not to fell to fcavengers and clowns,
But given to worthy perfons of renown.
        The number's few I've printed, in regard
My charges have been great, and I hope reward;
I caus'd not print many above twelve fcore,
And the printers are engag'd that they fhall print
        no more.

A a   APPEN-

APPENDIX.

FAMILY OF BUCCLEUGH.

OUR Author having traced the defcent of this honourable Family to the *Duke of Monmouth* (Part I. page 61.), we fhall now, following *Douglas*, in his Peerage of Scotland, give the fucceffion from that unfortunate nobleman to the prefent *Duke of Buccleugh*.

THE DUKE OF MONMOUTH was beheaded on Tower-hill the 15th July 1685, leaving iffue by the Dutchefs of Buccleugh four fons.

1. *Charles*, Earl of ·Doncafter, born in 1672, and died young. 2. *James*, born in 1674, who, after his father's attainder, was called Earl of Dalkeith, and carried on the line of this family. 3. *Henry*, born in 1676, created Earl of Deloraine. 4. *Francis*, born in 1678, and died young.

The Dutchefs-dowager of Monmouth and Buccleugh, in 1688, married to Charles Lord Cornwallis, by whom fhe had a fon, *George*, who died young,——and two daughters, 1. Lady *Anne*, who alfo died young. 2. Lady *Ifabella*.

The Dutchefs died in 1732, in the eighty-firft year of her age.

JAMES, Earl of Dalkeith, fon of the Duke of Monmouth, and Dutchefs of Buccleugh, married Lady Henriet Hyde, daughter of Laurence Earl of Rochefter, by whom he had three fons and two daughters.

1. *Francis*, his heir. 2. *James*, who died young. 3. *Henry*, who alfo died young.

His daughters, Lady *Anne* and Lady *Charlotte* died unmarried.

He

He was made knight of the thiſtle in 1703, and dying in 1704, was ſucceeded by his ſon,

FRANCIS, Earl of Dalkeith, who was made knight of the thiſtle in 1724, and ſucceeded to the honours and title of Duke of Buccleugh, upon the death of his grandmother, the Dutcheſs, *anno* 1732, and was choſen one of the ſixteen Peers for Scotland to the next *Britiſh* Parliament.

In 1743, he was reſtored to two of the Duke of Monmouth's titles, by act of Parliament, *viz.* Earl of Doncaſter, and Baron Scott of Tyndale, by which he became a Britiſh Peer.

In 1720, he married Lady Jane Douglas, daughter of James Duke of Queenſberry, by whom he had two ſons and three daughters.

1. *Francis*, Earl of Dalkeith. 2. *Charles*, who died unmarried at Oxford, in 1747.

1ſt daughter, Lady *Anne*. 2. Lady *Jane*. 3. Lady *Mary*.

He died 22d April 1751.

FRANCIS, Earl of Dalkeith, eldeſt ſon of Francis Duke of Buccleugh, in 1742, married Lady Caroline Campbell, eldeſt daughter of John duke of Argyle; by whom he had four ſons and two daughters.

1. *John*, Lord Whitcheſter, who died young. 2. *Henry*, the preſent Duke of Buccleugh. 3. *Campbell Scott*. 4. *James*, who died young.

1ſt. daughter, Lady *Caroline*. 2. Lady *Frances*, born after her father's death.

He died in April 1750, and was ſucceeded by his ſon.

HENRY, who ſucceeded alſo to his grandfather *anno* 1751, and is now Duke of Buccleugh, Earl of Dalkeith, Lord Whitcheſter, Baron Scott of Buccleugh and Eſkdale, in Scotland; and a Peer of England by the titles of Baron Tyndale in Northumberland, and Earl of Doncaſter in Yorkſhire, *&c.*

In

In 1767, he married Lady Elizabeth Montague, daughter to the Duke of Montague, by whom he has two sons and four daughters.

   1. *Charles* Earl of Dalkeith. 2. Lord *Henry.*

   1st daughter, Lady *Mary.* 2. Lady *Elizabeth.* 3. Lady *Caroline.* 4. Lady *Henriet.*

CHARACTER

OF

HENRY, DUKE OF BUCCLEUGH.

TO give a juſt portrait of one that no longer exiſts is con-feſſedly difficult. But fully to inveſtigate the character of an illuſtrious and virtuous nobleman, the living ornament of his country, would be a taſk of ſtill greater importance.——The editor, ſenſible of his inability to do juſtice to that cha-racter which all reſpect and admire, ſhall only, in compliance with his engagement to the public, endeavour to ſketch a few of its outlines.

THOUGH the private virtues of his Grace the Duke of Buccleugh might be exhibited in beautiful colours, and held up for the imitation of the great; yet, paſſing theſe, we ſhall on-ly take notice of a few things in his public character which are known facts, and will be allowed evidences of a good and ge-nerous heart.

A PREDILECTION for the country, and reſpect for the me-mory of his anceſtors, ſoon diſcovered themſelves in this great man; who, at a very early period, prov'd himſelf every way worthy of his illuſtrious deſcent.

His

His Grace's attachment to Scotland is the more to be ad-mired, when we reflect that England gave him birth and the principal part of his education, with an amiable partner for life—and that too ere he had well come of age. It was not till after the celebration of the nuptials that, with his confort, he vifited this country.

Having fix'd his principal refidence at Dalkeith, his Grace foon gave proofs of a fteady friendfhip for Scotland, by afford-ing the warmeft fupport to her trade and manufactures; and by giving every aid to the eftablifhment of a Bank, which, from its conftitution, he was fatisfied would be of public utili-ty; as no doubt it would, had the principles of honour and œconomy been ftrictly adhered to. But, in the end, both he and the nation were much difappointed.

His Grace, like a true patriot, hath ever been ready to a-vow his political fentiments, when duty or neceffity required. Nor has he hitherto attached himfelf to any party, further than he believed their conduct confiftent with the welfare of the State. We find him, upon various occafions, oppofing the Minifter, and exerting himfelf to counteract the fchemes of thofe, who, by fecret influence, endeavoured to clog the wheels of election,—depriving not only the commoners, but even the great men in the nation of the facred right which nature has given, and the precious bleffings which liberty beftows; and this too at a time when many of our nobles were yielding them-felves the tools of a party, and joyfully embracing the gilded bait!

Notwithstanding his oppofition to Minifters, his Grace withdrew not himfelf when the neceffities of the ftate and the fafety of the kingdom call'd for his aid. Then the heroic fpirit of the ancient Scotts, and the bravery of the Lords of Buccleugh, were found ftill alive in the chief of that honourable name, and noble defcendant of that illuftrious fa-mily. To fecure the peace of his country, and repel the

threaten'd

threaten'd invafion of her perfidious foe, the patriotic SCOTT was feen at the head of a regiment raifed by himfelf, and moftly compofed of volunteers from his own eftates, who, like the dependents of Buccleugh in every age, crowded to the ftandard of their chief,—not counting their blood to great a price for the liberty and profperity of their country. Having been raifed for the defence of Scotland alone, the *Southern Fencibles* never had an opportunity of fignalizing themfelves in the field. While the regiment exifted, his Grace, like a brave commander, was feldom abfent from head quarters, always attentive to duty, and ever ready to fhare with his men in the hardfhips of the march or the camp. The falling tear, when the government order for difbanding the regiment was read, demonftrated, more forcibly than any words, the gratitude of the foldiers, and the regard they had for their commander ; and his Grace's affurance of future friendfhip to fuch of them as might ftand in need of his affiftance, befpoke a generous and feeling heart, and prov'd affection to be reciprocal.

As a Superior, or Landlord, it will be found that the Duke of Buccleugh has indeed few equals. Under what great man are the tenants more wealthy, or of longer ftanding? The predeceffors of fome have occupied the fame farms for centuries paft. As a proof that all do well, none are inclin'd to remove. While the tenants rejoice in being under fuch a worthy nobleman, his Grace feels fatisfaction in beholding their profperity. ——If at any time, on account of a numerous family or unforefeen calmity, a tenant has fallen behind with the world, his Grace hath ever been ready, not to opprefs, but to provide for his neceffities.

UNIVERSAL BENEVOLENCE will be allowed the prefidency amongft the Chriftian graces. And where is there a brighter difplay of that virtue than in this great character? The nation can produce few equals. In this, his illuftrious confort,

the

the amiable Montague, may vie with him,—and to her who
holds his heart his Grace will be proud to yield the laurel.——
The Duke and Dutchess of Buccleugh think not, like many,
that to fee the poor daily thronging their gate detracts from
their dignity. No; their constant practice demonstrates the joy
they feel in relieving their fellow-creatures deprefs'd with poverty and bending under the infirmities of old age.——Afk
the poor in and around Dalkeith, who it is that daily relieves
their wants?—Afk the needy houfeholder, from whom he re-
ceives his weekly aliment?—Afk the family fuddenly overtaken
with diftrefs, or difappointments in trade, who anfwers their
petitions? Each tongue will reply, " *The Duke;*" or, *The
Dutchefs;*" and every heart join in imploring the bleffings
of heaven upon the noble pair and their promifing offspring.

    HAPPY would it be for Scotland, were all her nobility pof-
fefs'd of thofe eminent virtues that appear in their Graces of
Buccleugh. The nation might then rejoice, and the heart now
prefs'd with the iron hand of poverty might exult, looking
forward to more joyful days.

──────────────

The following VERSES on his Grace the Duke of BUC-
CLEUGH'S *Birth-day, copied from the* Scots Magazine *for*
1767, *we prefume will not be unacceptable to the reader.*

WHERE Melrofe fane in ruin'd beauty ftands,
        The work of pious and of impious hands,
Old Father TWEED from off his pebbly bed,
This morn, hoarfe murmuring rais'd his watry head.
    What means, my fons, with angry voice he cried,
This frantic riot that difturbs my tide?
Peaceful, tho' dull, for many years I've lain,
Unftain'd by lovers or by warriors flain;

                                            But

But now my hills with joyful fhouts refound,
And gladnefs revels o'er my claffic ground.
My rural *Etrick*, fee, in mantle gay,
With dancing pace comes on his fhining way;
My tragic *Yarrow* cafts his mournful weeds,
And like a mafker trips it down the meads.
While here in calm forgetfulnefs I lay,
What fhame to wake me with this antic fray?
For fhame, my fons! Tell *Etrick, Yarrow* tell!
What rage, what phrenfy, does your bofoms fwell?

  Yarrow, the rapture glowing in his eyes,
With fpeedy words thus to his fire replies.
Roll, Father TWEED! roll on your filver ftreams,
With double fplendor fhine in funny beams,
To where the *Tiviot* down his pleafant dale
Makes hafte to meet thee with a joyful tale.
A SCOTT, a Noble SCOTT! again appears,
The wifh'd for blefting of thy hoary years!
Hark! how th' impetuous *Efk* in thunder roars!
Hark! how the foaming *Liddal* beats his fhores!
A SCOTT, a SCOTT! triumphantly they cry!
A SCOTT, a SCOTT! a thoufand hills reply!
The night is paft, again the day's at hand,
To light this dark, and long deferted land.
Be glad ye hills! rejoice each living fpring!
Ye Mufes wake! and every Valley fing!

  ILLUSTRIOUS YOUTH! trace back the rolls of fame,
Perufe the annals of thy warlike name;
Cull the beft honours of thy noble race,
Join to SCOTT's daring genius, MONMOUTH's grace;
Add, if thou wilt, the ftrennous DOUGLAS' ire,
And temper all with CAMPBELL's patriot fire:
Yet 'midft the glories of thy princely line,
The virtues of humanity be thine!
Our haplefs land in vain has long complain'd,
Of chiefs in fyren bondage ftill detain'd:

Idly

Idly in courts who wafte their tedious days,
Afleep alike to pleafure and to praife.
Break thou the charm ! with merit all thine own,
Seek an untroden path to high renown !
   Be thine, Fair MONTAGUE, the gen'rous part,
To aid the purpofe of a patriot heart.
Be this thy country ! thou her pride and boaft !
And full repay her the long years fhe's loft.
So fhall the ftreamy South revere thy name,
And tafk her mufes to exalt thy fame.
So fhall kind Heaven in all propitious prove,
Preferve thy glory, and reward thy love.

   TWEED-SIDE, Sept. 13. 1767.

The following note was omitted on page 14. Part I. where Satchels tells
  us that the houfe of Haffendean was the moft ancient branch from
  Scott of Buccleugh.

   At what period the male line of this family failed we cannot certainly
determine. But it is fome time fince the lands of Haffendean, which
are extenfive, returned, by purchafe, to the family of Buccleugh. David
Scott, the firft that we find defigned of Haffendean was eldeft fon of Sir
Walter Scott of Kirkurd, who, in 1446, exchanged his lands of Murdiefton for the lands of Branxholm, &c. as note on page 46, Part I. The
family of Haffendean being now extinct the reprefentation devolves to
William Scott of Burnhead and Crowhill, as lineal male defcendant of
the firft John Scott of Burnhead, younger brother of David of Haffendean, and fecond fon to the above Sir Walter Scott of Kirkurd. Vide
Douglas's Peerage, page 101.

MEMOIRS

MEMOIRS

OF THE

LIFE AND MILITARY SERVICES

O F

LIEUTENANT-GENERAL ELLIOT.

SIR GEORGE-AUGUSTUS ELLIOT, the brave and gallant defender of Gibralter, is the fon of the late Sir Gilbert Elliot, Bart. of Stobs, in Roxburghfhire.——The an- cient and honourable family of Elliot of Stobs, as well as the col- lateral branch of Elliot of Minto in the fame county, and of El- liot of Port-Elliot in Cornwall, are originally from Normandy. Their anceftor, Mr Alliot, came over with William the Con- queror, and held a diftinguifhed rank in his army. There is a traditional anecdote in the family, relating to an honourable diftinction-in their Coat of Arms, which, as it correfponds with hiftory *, bears the appearance of truth. When the Conqueror fet foot on the Englifh land, he ftumbled and fell on the earth. He immediately fprung up and exclaimed, that it was a happy omen, he had embraced the country of which he was to be- come the fovereign. Upon this Alliot drew his fword, and fwore by the honour of a foldier, that he would maintain, at the hazard of his blood, the right of his Lord to the fove- reignty of the earth which he had embraced. On the event of conqueft, William added to the arms of Alliot, which was a batten *or*, on a field *azure*, the *arm* and *fword* as a creft, with the motto, *Per faxa, per ignes, fortiter et recte.*

* Hume's Hiftory of England.

Sir

Sir Gilbert Elliot of Stobs had nine sons and two daughters.   The present General was the youngest son, and he is
now the only surviving one. -His eldest brother, Sir John, left
the title and estate to his son the present Sir Francis Elliot,
who is nephew to the General. -- ;

George-Augustus Elliot was born about the year
1718, and received the rudiments of his education under a
private tutor retained in the family.   At an early age he was
sent to the University of Leyden, where he made a rapid progress in classical learning, and spoke with elegance and fluency
the German and French languages.- Being designed for a military life, he was sent from thence to the celebrated *Ecole Roy-
ale du genie militaire,* at La Fere in Picardy.   This school
was the most famous in Europe, by means of the great Vaubon
by whom it was conducted.   Here it was that the foundation
was laid of that knowledge of tactics in all its branches, and
particularly in the arts of engineering and fortification, which
has since so greatly distinguished this Officer. He completed his
military course on the continent by a tour, for the purpose of
seeing in practice what he had studied in theory.   Prussia was
the model for discipline, and he continued sometime as a volunteer in that service.   Such were the steps taken by the
young men of fashion in that day, to accomplish themselves for
the service of their country.

Mr Elliot returned in the 17th year of his age to his native country, Scotland; and was the same year, 1735, introduced
by his father, Sir Gilbert, to Lieutenant-Colonel Peers of the 23d
regiment of foot, then lying at Edinburgh, as a youth anxious
to bear arms for his king and country.   He was accordingly
entered as a volunteer in that regiment and continued for a
year or more.   At this time he gave prelude of his future military talents, and showed that he was at least a soldier *au coeur.*
From the 23d he went into the Engineer Corps at Woolwich,
and made great progress in that study, until his uncle, Colonel

Elliot,

Elliot, brought him in as Adjutant in the second troop of Horfe Grenadiers. In this fituation he conducted himfelf with the moft examplary attention, and laid the foundation of that. difcipline which has rendered thefe two troops the fineft corps of heavy Cavalry in Europe; with thefe troops he went upon fervice to Germany in the war before laft and was with them in a variety of actions. At the battle of Dittengen he was wounded. In this corps he firft bought the rank of Captain and Major, and afterwards purchafed the Lieutenant-Colonelcy from Colonel Brewerton, who fucceeded to his uncle. On arriving at this rank he refigned his commiffion as an engineer, which he had enjoyed along with his other rank, and in which fervice he had been actively employed, very much to the advantage of his country. He had received the inftructions of the famous Engineer Beltidor, and made himfelf completely mafter of the Science of Gunnery. Had he not difintereftedly refigned his rank in the Engineer department, he would now, by regular progreffion, have been at the head of that corps. Soon after this he was appointed Aid de-Camp to King George II. and was already diftinguifhed for his military fkill and difcipline. In the year 1759, he quitted the fecond troop of Horfe Grenadier Guards, being felected to raife, form, and difcipline the firft regiment of Light Horfe, called after him, *Elliot's*. As foon as they were raifed and formed, he was appointed to the command of the Cavalry in the expedition on the coafts of France, with the rank of Brigadier-General. After this he paffed into Germany, where he was employed on the Staff, and greatly diftinguifhed himfelf in a variety of movements, while his regiment difplayed a ftrictnefs of difcipline, an activity, and enterprize, which gained them fignal honour.——From Germany he was recalled, for the purpofe of being employed as fecond in command in the memorable expedition againft the Havannah. It was poffible to find an officer in the funfhine of the Court, to whom, under the patronage of a prince, the trappings of the chief command might be given; but an Elliot was wanted to act, as well as an Albemarle to fhine, and for him they were obliged to go to the dufty plains of Germany. The circumftances of that conqueft are well known. It feems as if our brave veteran had always in his eye the gallant Lewis de Velafco, who maintained his ftation to the laft extremity, and, when his garrifon were flying from his fide or falling at his feet, difdained to call for quarter, but fell glorioufly—exercifing his fword upon his conquerors.

THE reader will pardon the recital of a fhort anecdote, which occurred immediately after the reduction of that fortrefs, as it fhows, that in the very heat and outrage of war, the General was not unmindful of the rights of humanity.—— He was particularly eminent among the conquerors of the Havannah, for his difinterefted procedure, and for his checking the horrors of indifcriminate plunder. To him therefore appeals were moft frequently made. A Frenchman, who had fuffered greatly by the depredations of the foldiery, made application to him, and begged, in bad Englifh, that he would interfere to have his property reftored. The petitioner's wife, who was prefent, a woman of great fpirit, was angry at her hufband for his interceffion, and faid, " Comment " pouvez vous demander du grace a un homme qui vient vous " depouiller? N'en esperez pas *." The hufband perfifting in his application, his wife grew more loud in the cenfure, and faid, " Vous n'etes pas François †!" The General, who was bufy writing at the time, turned to the woman, and faid, fmiling, " Madam, ne vous echauffez pas, ce que votre mari " demande lui fera acorde ‡."—" Oh faut-il pour furcroit de " malheur," exclaimed the woman, " que le barbare parle le " François §." The General was fo very much pleafed with the woman's fpirit, that he not only procured them their pro-

---

* How can you afk a favour from a man who comes to rob you? Do not hope for it.   † You are not a Frenchman.   ‡ Madam, don't put yourfelf in a paffion, what your hufband afks fhall be granted him.
§ O what an addition to my misfortune, that the barbarian fpeaks French!

perty

perty again, but alfo took pains to accommodate them in e-
very refpect.   This has been through life the manly character
of the General.   If he would not fuffer his foldiers, for the
fake of plunder, to extend the ravages of war, he never impo-
verifhed them by unjuft exactions.   He would not confent that
his Quarter-mafter's place fhould be fold, " not only," fays
he, " becaufe I think it the reward of an honeft veteran ; but
" alfo becaufe I could not exercife my authority in his difmif-
" fion fhould he behave ill."

ON the peace his gallant regiment was reviewed by the
King, when they prefented to his Majefty the ftandards which
they had taken from the enemy.   Gratified with their fine difcipline and high character, the King afked General Elliot what
mark of his favour he could beftow on his regiment equal to
their merit.   He anfwered, that his regiment would be proud,
if his Majefty fhould think, that, by their fervices, they were
entitled to the diftinction of *Royals*.   It was accordingly made
a royal regiment, with this flattering title, " The 15th, or
" *King's* royal regiment of Light Dragoon's."   At the fame
time the King expreffed a defire to confer fome honour on the
General himfelf; but he declared, that the honour and fatisfaction of his Majefty's approbation of his fervices was his beft
reward.

DURING the peace he was not idle.   His great talents in
the curious branches of the military art, gave him ample em-
ployment.   In the year 1775, he was appointed to fucceed
General A'Court, as Commander in Chief of the forces in
Ireland.   But did not continue long in this ftation; not even
fo long as fully to unpack all his trunks; for, finding that in-
terferences were made by authority derogatory of his own, he
refifted the practice with becoming fpirit; and, not chufing to
difturb the government of that kingdom on a matter perfonal
to himfelf, he folicited to be recalled, and accordingly was fo,
when

when he was appointed to the command of Gibraltar, in a fortunate hour for the safety of that important fortress.

THE gallant defence made by the General, against the united forces of France and Spain, during a blockade and siege for upwards of three years, is not equalled in the annals of Britain. The system of his life, as well as his education, peculiarly qualified him for this important trust. He is perhaps the most abstemious man of the age. His food vegetables and his drink water; seldom or never indulging himself in animal food nor wine. He never sleeps more than four hours at a time. So inured to habits of hardiness, that what is painful to other men is natural and easy to him. His wants easily supplied, and his watchfulness beyond precedent. His example had a most persuasive efficacy on the brave troops in the garrison. Like him, they regulated their lives by the strictest rules of discipline; and severe exercise with short diet became habitual to them by their own choice. The preparations which he made for his defence, were contrived with so much judgment, and executed with such address, that, with a handful of men, he defended that garrison against an attack which would have been sufficient to exhaust any common set of men. Collected within himself, he never spent his ammunition in useless parade or unimportant attacks. The cool intrepidity he discovered on the ever-memorable 13th of September 1782, when the grand attack was made by the enemy, with forty-four sail of the line, ten battering ships, five bomb-ketches, several gun and mortar boats, a large floating-battery, a number of armed vessels, and near three hundred boats constructed for carrying troops,—their land-batteries mounted with above one hundred pieces of canon, and an equal number of mortars and howitzers, with an army of near forty thousand men, procured him the approbation of every individual of his gallant troops, who were eye witnesses of his conduct, and who shared with him in the dangers and glory of the day: And the new-invented method by which he
brought

brought deftruction on that formidable force, and terminated the afpiring hopes of the enemy, will be recorded to the lateft generations, to the immortal honour of the Britifh arms, and the lafting glory of the intrepid Elliot.

Soon after this memorable event, both houfes of Parliament voted an unanimous addrefs of thanks to the General ; and his Majefty conferred on him the honour of Knight of the Bath, with a penfion of *L.* 1500 *per annum*, during his own life, and that of his fon.

The General continues Governor of Gibraltar ; where it is thought he will remain till the works now going forward, under his direction, tending to ftrengthen that fortrefs, are completed.

Though he is now in the fixty-eighth year of his age, and has fpent a great part of his life in fevere difcipline in fultry climates, and in hard ftruggles for the honour of his king and country, his temperate living has procured him a good ftate of health, and preferved his looks with great frefhnefs.

General Elliot married a fifter of the prefent Sir Francis Drake; by whom he has a fon, at prefent Lieutenant-Colonel in the Innifkilling Dragoons; and a daughter, married to Mr Fuller of Bayley Park in Suffex. His Lady died about feventeen years ago.

T H E   E N D.

THE INDEX.

PART FIRST.

PART SECOND.

The INDEX.

www.ingramcontent.com/pod-product-compliance
Lightning Source LLC
Chambersburg PA
CBHW020613030726
47497CB00007B/2221